The Peach Tree
Family Cookbook

by
Cynthia Collins Pedregon
The Peach Tree Gift Gallery and Tea Room
Fredericksburg, Texas

Cover Design & Illustrations
by
Becky Crouch Patterson

Photos by
Lynn A. Herrmann

© 1994 Lynn A. Herrmann

Copyright © 1994
by
Peach Tree Gift Gallery & Tea Room
210 South Adams Street
Fredericksburg, Texas 78624
(210) 997-9527

ISBN 0-9627590-0-7
Library of Congress Catalog Card # 94-066692

Printed in the USA by
WIMMER BROTHERS
A Wimmer Company
Memphis • Dallas

Dedication

to my parents
Enid and Frederic Collins
for all the memories
d cherish
♡

History of The Peach Tree

Three and a half years have passed since we published our first book "The Peach Tree Tea Room Cookbook" and much has happened in the life of The Peach Tree.

About four weeks after our book was finished, Cynthia's mother, Enid Collins, passed away suddenly. Enid did the calligraphy for the book and was our main critic and encourager. In her own right, Enid was a fine designer, creating beautiful things in stitcheries, pottery, handbags, needlepoint - with a national reputation for her work. So, we were blessed to have her guidance and encouragement as Cynthia developed that first book. She lived to see the final product and was so excited for us at the overwhelming reception the book received. We are grateful to her for her loving support and affirmation.

In the spring of 1991, a dear friend joined our company, Tom Richards. Tom is a CPA who had been the financial officer for eleven years of a very large jewelry firm in Kerrville. At the time, we so desperately needed someone we could trust and depend on to take over the office operations of our expanding business. He relieved us of these pressures so that Cynthia and I could concentrate on product development. Tom has been a very important part of our team and we are grateful to have him in our Peach Tree family.

Also in 1991, we added "The Peach Tree On Main" - our downtown store - specializing in books, cards and gifts. We had not considered another store in Fredericksburg until my brother-in-law, Jeep Collins, wanted to open a location for his company at the new BankOne building and wanted a "familiar neighbor" in the location next to his. The decision to open that store was very rewarding, and it gave us a fresh new direction in merchandising our stores.

Judy Morgan, our former manager, who was so instrumental in helping us develop and produce the first book, retired last year and is enjoying the pleasures that life brings. Sandy Nigh, joined our firm last summer as our new manager, and has brought an exciting energy into our company. We had known Sandy for several years as a representative for major product lines at the Dallas Trade Center before coming here. Her background and experience have been an enormous help in guiding our day-to-day operations. It's nice to have her on our team now.

In March of this year, we started the expansion of our Tea Room which will virtually double our capacity. Since our small kitchen was not able to produce enough foods to accommodate the large numbers of people we were serving daily, the expansion came quite naturally.

Also, with our plans to expand the kitchen, we had an opportunity to increase our seating capacity. In addition, we added a Deli counter, which will specialize in new and exciting foods to go. This idea was born of requests from customers wanting foods for entertaining and from the many people who stay in our local bed and breakfast homes, who come to enjoy the city, but do not want to spend a great deal of time in food preparation. We are excited about this new addition, because it will give us an opportunity to prepare many different kinds of foods which we do not normally serve daily in our Tea Room.

Which brings me to the present, Cynthia's second book "The Peach Tree Family Cookbook." My goodness ... we never dreamed we would produce another book. After our first experience, it was the furthest thing from our minds. On that book, we labored for four years - writing, compiling, editing, computerizing, photographing - to pull together what had always been a dream of Cynthia's, to gather a collection of our Tea Room recipes into a book. Our customers had encouraged her to do it!

As our project progressed on that book, I recall discussing the publication of 5,000 copies because we felt it was a financially manageable amount for us to handle. However, when the Wimmer Company, our publisher, reviewed the book, they highly encouraged us to print 10,000 because they felt we had a winner. You can imagine our surprise! How could they be so sure - we had never produced a book before - we had no track record! And what if they were wrong? What does one do with 10,000 copies of a cookbook if it doesn't sell? After a string of prayers, our instinct was to go with their advice. They proved themselves right after we sold the first 5,000 copies in eight weeks! We were so grateful to have the other 5,000 copies to carry us until our second printing. Thanks to our customers and people everywhere, we have printed books every year and will print our fourth edition this year - which will total 37,500 copies printed to date! The book is now marketed nationally.

Cynthia has received many wonderful and encouraging notes from customers everywhere - telling her how much they have enjoyed her book. Most comment on how easy the recipes are to follow and how good the foods turn out -- exactly what Cynthia had hoped for. It was this type of "applause" that convinced her to produce this second book.

In the last three and a half years, Cynthia had created enough recipes to fill another book from foods used in our Tea Room and our many caterings. This book, however, is a collection of these recipes plus old family recipes and some very special ones from good friends -- one reason this book is larger than the first.

It has been a labor of love for Cynthia since our daughter, Tina, was involved in helping write this book. Tina finished her degree in Communications and was very instrumental in helping computerize some of Cynthia's early work. Tina also has the same love of foods as her mother. She developed many of the cookie and pizza recipes in this book. It was a joy to see them working together side by side as the book developed. Tina is now our kitchen manager and doing a tremendous job!

As an update on the rest of our family - our son, David, who worked with us for so many years, is now an investment consultant at BankOne in Fredericksburg. Last January, he married our precious Helana, a delight to our family. Our musically-talented son, Carlos, is living in Austin pursuing a career in music.

It seems we leapfrog through life -- compressing groups of years as though they were one. Yet, as I reflect, there have been so many good family times of sharing, seeing our children grow and gratefully, all of us, still in our beloved, Fredericksburg. Yes, the Lord is gracious! He truly has given us more than we deserve and more than we ever anticipated.

May you enjoy this book which was born of the love of Cynthia and Tina, our many friends and our encouraging staff at The Peach Tree. And may we have the pleasure of your visits to our shops and Tea Room when you visit our city.

Gratefully,

Hector

Once upon a time I planned to be
an artist of celebrity.
A song I thought to write one day,
and all the world would homage pay.
But what I did – was learn to cook.
For life with simple tasks is filled.
And I have done, not what I willed,
yet when I see boys' hungry eyes
I'm glad I make good
apple pies!

FROM CYNTHIA'S HEART

To all of my Peach Tree kitchen companions - for the recipe testing and testing... and testing... - I truly appreciate your patience and your affirming love.

My heart is full of gratitude to all of you who have been so appreciative of my first book - I received such sweet affirming notes and phone calls from you - Thanks.

Peggy Cox was our kitchen manager for a time - during which we had the joy of cooking and catering together and developing new recipes. We did the Black-eyed Pea and Ham together for New Year's eve in the Tea Room - the Butternut Squash was Peggy's contribution to those who prefer low fat foods - Chicken and Barley has become a favorite with just about everybody! Thanks to Peggy for the sweet memories!

Also to Babs Parrott, my wonderful encourager, who spent end-less hours at the computer making certain that every new recipe I did was safely stored in her computer program. And to Tom Richards, our CFO, who orchestrated the computer programs and layouts and also spent so many hours making sure everything was done right.

One of my great joys in life is preparing food and creating new ways to combine flavors - presenting and sharing with friends. A special thanks to my good friend, Loretta Schmidt, for her ability to translate my actions into legible instructions.

Dr. Charles Schmidt, my good friend of many years, who is a dentist by day - and at other times one of the best cooks I've ever met! I feel privileged to have a collection of his "tried and delicious" recipes included in my book. They are all treasures - the Electra Sorbet may be my new favorite dessert!

My heart felt thanks go to Marianne and Steve Sprinkle for their new friendship. Their small organic vegetable farm located in Dripping Springs has been a tremendous inspiration to me in the past year.

On the eve of our photo shoot, I picked up an ordinary brown box at the bus station from Steve and Marianne. It was still very early spring in Fredericksburg and our gardens weren't producing yet, so I had asked them to send me what they could for my garnishes. When I got home and opened the box I felt like I had found a treasure chest - it was filled to the brim with some of the most beautiful freshly picked bounty I'd ever seen. One by one I took out the carefully tied bundles of herbs and greens - rosemary, thyme, oregano, Italian parsley, salad burnet, basil, chard, mustard ... floral bunches of calendula, violas, johnny jump-ups, arugula flowers. I placed them in vases on my kitchen table - it was a visual feast for one such as I who loves to find new ideas to garnish and trim platters - platter paint. Enclosed was a sweet note of encouragement ... instead of a bill! Notice how we used these treasures to garnish for the pictures. Thanks to Marianne and Steve for the inspiration your labors have given me and for your cherished friendship.

Joanie Harris - for all the fine editing skills, and her ability to clarify my phrases - in effect, to read and interpret my heart.

To my precious daughter, Tina, who returned home from college with her degree in communications just in time to encourage me in this awesome challenge of writing another cookbook. God does His work in mighty and wondrous ways. I give God thanks for this year and a half that Tina and I have spent working closely together developing new recipes. She is a wonderful cook, has fine writing and editing skills, and she has a strong sense of design. Most of all she's just one of my best friends in all the world!

To Hector, who I think always knew there would be another book. He made certain that all the newly developed recipes went into the computer without fail - for which I'm grateful. My tendency is to make a dish - then I go on to a new creative challenge. Hector's sense of order has placed a welcomed demand on me to be more disciplined and to record all of my recipes just as they are done.

Our life together is exciting, sometimes filled with almost more activity than I can handle. Thank God I'm married to a fine and wonderful man, who in the midst of our sometimes whirlwind - no, tornado - of activity, values me as his wife more than his business partner. As my husband, Hector has the ability to provide a haven and a stability which blesses and settles me in a way that no business partner ever could.

To my heavenly father, my heart is full of gratitude and wonder that you would heap such abundant blessing on my life. I marvel that you would provide such beauty for us to enjoy in our surroundings and in our relationships. For sending us your Holy Spirit to provide the *salt and flavor that makes our life so rich - Thank you my father, my Lord!

To Mime - how I miss you... and I hope you and the angels are smiling at the release of this book, too!

*Let me tell you why you are here. You're here to be salt - seasoning that brings out the God flavors of this earth. If you lose your saltiness, how will people taste godliness? - Matt 5:13

A NOTE FROM CYNTHIA

I have a good friend whom I don't see very often - but when we do get together Barbara Bailey Gaines and I always end up talking about recipes and entertaining - whether it's for our immediate families or for a party of several hundred. Barbara was the social director for the president of the University of Texas. She traveled all over the country organizing parties for the University. One time we discussed the important role that food and its presentation play in setting the stage for people to be together. For Barbara, that has involved setting the stage for important dignitaries to get together to make far reaching decisions - sometimes there were parties held in elegant ballrooms and sometimes parties on sandy, windy beaches. I particularly admire Barbara's talent for flower arranging - she creates gorgeous arrangements as back drops when she gives parties. Equally as important to Barbara is the presentation of nourishing food to her husband and two sons in her cozy country kitchen. Barbara and I readily affirm one another in this common gift we share.

Since our conversation that day I've spent lots of thinking time considering how my love of cooking for others developed. Our lives are somewhat like puzzles made up of many pieces - contributed by many people. My thoughts have turned to those who have had an influence on my direction.

I grew up on a small ranch in the Texas Hill Country. Our home was located 14 miles from the small community of Medina - population 400. My parents bought the land, sight unseen, with their war bonds while they were living in Detroit during the war. Together, and with the help of two other men, they built our home themselves. My dad's lifelong dream was to be a cowboy and live in Texas! In my early years, growing up in our secluded country home, I was sure that I belonged to a very elegant family because even for the simplest of occasions my mother went to great lengths to prepare for company. Our entertaining included my grandparents and a very small circle of friends - not a grand number of people - but the few visitors that came to our home in those early days knew that their presence was important to us.

My mother was my earliest source of encouragement and the one who most influenced the direction of the family's life-style. I remember the many times as a little girl when she would involve us in preparing for holidays. One of the first signs of an approaching holiday was evidenced by her spreading the family silver out on the dining table.

My little brother, Jeep, and I would carefully remove every bit of the tarnish until the silver gleamed. The excitement would grow in my spirit as the house would be dusted, floors would be waxed, and flowers or branches of natural foliage were brought in from the pasture to decorate our home.

When the house was company-ready, then the food preparation began. I can't remember a time when I wasn't involved in that part. I began by arranging relishes - with Mom's watchful eye, I'm sure. She taught me that it didn't take a lot of time or money to make things look pretty - just care and the desire to please and delight those we were serving.

By the time my grandparents, aunts and uncles arrived I was ready to pop with the excitement of it all. Easter, Thanksgiving, Christmas, and *everyone's* birthday were important in our family. These were occasions when all else was set aside so we could enjoy being with each other. Gathering around the table was always central to the day's events!

My dad also influenced me in developing a sense of hospitality. He grew up in a very elegant home where the family "dressed for dinner." Even in the days after the great depression when my grandfather lost his business, the Collins family maintained a sense of order and family dignity. My parents instilled a real appreciation in us to respect others' feelings, and manners were taught to us at an early age. I smile - remembering how my father once admonished my brother at our table to maintain a "semblance of nicety." My brother responded with, "A what?!" and then proceeded to fall off his chair onto the floor, convulsed into giggles (like the rest of us)! My dad's good influence prevailed, and my brother and I both learned from our parents that manners were important because they were a way of expressing respect for others - and hospitality was a way of showing care and appreciation for others.

Being born into an artistic family can be confusing. How well I remember being somewhat frustrated when I didn't enjoy painting classes. I really felt detached as a Collins when my drawing and designing skills didn't develop in me as I felt they should. I was sure I had not been born with an artistic gift like the rest of my family until I was "twenty something."

When Hector and I married and began our home life, we soon realized how much we both enjoyed entertaining. We preferred having friends in our home rather than going out. Hector has been my greatest source of affirmation in the area of my cooking. Even in the early days of our marriage he was totally encouraging and appreciative. I can't ever remember a complaint as I tried out all the new "creations" on him!

We've always felt that family mealtime was very important. In today's world it can be a challenge trying to maintain this tradition. I'm thankful that we agreed on the importance of a time together, set apart from the rest of the day, when we could focus on one another and enjoy each other while seated around our dining table.

Very recently I visited our family's cemetery in San Antonio and remembered the stories I'd heard from my mother and aunt about relatives that I barely knew. I realized what an impact our ancestors have on us as the memories are passed down through our family. Seeing the gravestone of my great grandmother, Mary Roessler, jolted my memory to the pies that my mother loved so much. Our Mother's Day tradition included Grandma's Caramel Pie and Chocolate Pie because my mother couldn't decide which of the two she preferred. Mime (my mother) told me often about going to Grandma's house on Sundays where the family would gather for dinner - each place was set with a slice of Caramel or Chocolate Pie - the promise of a delicious ending of the meal prepared by my great grandmother's loving hands.

I only knew my great grandmother from the visits to the nursing home after she was confined to her bed, but I experienced a special feeling of continuity with her that day at the cemetery - that she then, and I now, share the love of providing a setting where the senses of taste and hunger are satisfied and loved ones are made comfortable and content. Setting the stage for times of loving family communication and relationships was her passion and is mine also.

Discovering my gift for hospitality and giving myself into the enjoyment of it has been liberating for me. I don't invite someone into my home without suggesting some way to nourish them with food. Part of the comfort of entering a loving home to me is having the fragrance of nourishment present. God gave us the senses of smell and taste for our enjoyment - and for me it's an opportunity to give satisfaction and love.

We who entertain have a precious opportunity to more than just feed people - we can create an atmosphere for relationships to flourish. Dinner gatherings with friends, catering weddings, providing comfort food at funerals, preparing special homecoming meals for your son (and sometimes his girlfriend!), entertaining new in-laws, or even those cozy dinners for two - all these provide opportunities for people to get to know each other better. We who entertain have the ability to touch and affect others - to provide a setting and an atmosphere where bonding can take place. It's our chance to bless others in a powerful way.

I love the gift of hospitality that God gave me - it brings me the greatest joy when I'm able to share it with others. I hope this book gives you encouragement and joy as you read it. I hope it blesses you

14

also. Perhaps when you put this cookbook down you will find your heart touched and you will sense a spark of encouragement to experiment with and develop your own style of hospitality, to find the joy of preparing food and giving of yourself for others in a way that invites them to enjoy something a little more special than just eating another meal.

Stay on good terms with each other, held together by love. Be ready with a meal or a bed when it's needed. Why, some have extended hospitality to angels without ever knowing it! - Hebrews 13:2

Cynthia-age 6-with parents and a guest Medina Ranch 1952

A NOTE FROM TINA

Ever since I was a little girl, I've adored everything about Mom. She and Dad sent me to summer camp when I very young, and I can remember standing by the cabin watching Mom drive away in our family station wagon with big tears in my eyes because I knew how much I would miss her. She was just as weepy when she would give me a good-bye hug. I would tell her that I would much rather stay home and "play in the kitchen" with her. Mom has such a gift for nurturing family and friends - not surprisingly, it most often takes place in her kitchen - her domain. Her passion for food and entertaining enables her to bring joy to people close to her. My love of cooking certainly comes from my mother. I feel such gratitude for Mom's willingness to teach me how to cook and for instilling in me the same desire to nurture my family and friends.

While I was in summer school a couple of years ago, I spent a great deal of time cooking for my boyfriend and his twin brother. Somehow, we got into the habit of having pizza together several nights each week. David and Tim were creative in suggesting various ingredients and sometimes just appearing with a pound of shrimp or a beautiful fillet of salmon.

My first experience making pizza was incredibly time consuming. I had found a book on making pizzas and spent all afternoon gathering ingredients and preparing the dough and pizza sauce. The results were satisfying but the time involved was discouraging. After my first experience of making pizza, I decided to leave my pizza book on the shelf, and experiment on my own. I have simplified making pizza and learned how to lessen the time involved by breaking the process down into steps that make baking pizza more manageable and fun. Using a Cuisinart to make the dough, for example, combines mixing and kneading the dough into one step. It's not so intimidating to make dough this way. Making double batches of pizza sauce and freezing it is another way that I cut down on time.

My little brother, Carlos, lived with me in San Antonio during his freshman year in college. He had a great group of friends who would come over quite often to visit or play guitar. Whenever I offered to cook dinner for everyone, pizza would often be the preferred choice. With Carlos' carefree spirit, I usually didn't have much time to get something together. So I used my stored pizza sauce and grated cheeses from my freezer, along with Paletta's Hot Italian Sausage.

I wish I could count the times that I've been asked about the fat content in my pizzas. My guests are sometimes concerned that the pizza they are enjoying so much should be accompanied by guilt. Usually, I'm able to say that with the exception of some olive oil in the crust and sauce, the cheese is the main "no-no." Some cheeses are lower in fat than others, like Farmer's Cheese, or those made with skim or low-fat milk. Salmon and Brie Pizza probably won't help your waistline, but most of my pizzas are healthy and moderately low in fat.

The choices of ingredients to go into making a pizza can be end-less. Here, I have tried to include a range of different recipes to give an idea of what flavors work well together. The Eggplant and Prosciutto Pizza is one of my favorite pizzas because of the blend of special ingre-dients - eggplant with prosciutto, sauteed garlic, and crisp cornmeal crust blend fine, robust flavors. The Tomatillo y Pollo Pizza is my version of a Mexican pizza. I like the combination of green chilies with tomatillos and barbecue chicken with Monterey Jack cheese - jalapeños add just enough spark to make this pizza interesting.

Creating these pizza recipes has been so much fun. Having to write down specific quantities and putting ingredients together did not come easy for me since I never made the same pizza twice. I like to begin creating a pizza by starting with a fresh ingredient like ripe summer garden tomatoes or colored bell peppers, and experimenting with exotic cheeses and anything out of the ordinary.

During the writing of this cookbook, we were building an addition on to our Tea Room. The builders had been working extra long hours to get the construction finished on time and occasionally they would gather after work to wind down before going home. On one particular afternoon, I had baked four different types of pizza, testing for the cookbook. With more than our refrigerator and freezer could handle - due to all of the testing we had been doing - I decided to get some unbiased opinions and let them help "critique" my pizzas. I received all the thanks I needed from the sounds of satisfaction and smiles of approval on their faces.

Pizza can be a versatile entrée. I have served pizza for casual "get-togethers" on the patio with a pitcher of beer as well as in finer settings with a green salad and good wine. The Shrimp Pizza, for example, can be beautiful when served for elegant dinners, especially when the jumbo shrimp are arranged in the middle and garnished with freshly picked basil sprigs.

I enjoy creating an atmosphere of elegance when serving pizza because I've always felt that it was important to make simple occasions special. One way to do this is with little touches -- adding a few small sprigs of fresh herbs or edible nasturtium leaves and flowers on each plate gives color and a "bouquet" for the table. I set the table with linens and vintage silver, and light some candles.

I have never had the patience that mom has had in the kitchen - she thrives on spending hours cooking special meals. I also enjoy being in the kitchen, but my limited endurance there is related to my being such a goal oriented person! Most of us have busy schedules these days and little time to spend on long cooking processes. When I think of serving pizza, I think of surprising my guests with a gourmet pizza that has a wonderful homemade crust topped with fresh ingredients rather than the fast food version.

I hope that my pizza recipes can be a guide to show what has been successful for me so that you can have fun creating your own versions. Mom is talented in using ingredients available to her and substituting to make recipes her own. My pizza recipes are meant to be used in this way - to show what has been successful for me and as a guide for creating countless new pizzas for the experienced cook and for you who are just beginning! Enjoy!

Book Design

Becky Patterson and I have been friends for over 20 years, encouraging and admiring one another through life. We both grew up in the heart of the Texas Hill Country. Both of us the first born, daughters of very talented parents and both of us began learning early to combine the elegant with the primitive. Becky is one of the most brilliant and creative people I've ever met.

We are simpático. We like the same images - sheep, angels, hearts. We have both been influenced by the Mexican and German cultures. It was Becky's idea to collect Spanish dichos (sayings) and German proverbs from relatives and old timers. The tradition of the spoken words, her images and symbols feed our soul because they embody spirit, land, heart and hand. Just as I take care to decorate every plate I serve with fruit and flowers - so has Becky garnished every page with the flora and crafts - punched tin, crocheted lace, clay angels, quilt patterns, herbs and ivy topiaries - of our native Texans.

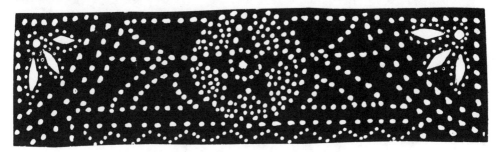

Table of Contents

Appetizers

Hot Artichoke Dip

An easy to do appetizer - it can be done ahead and refrigerated until party time - then popped in the oven just before your guests arrive. It's delicious - you will get lots of compliments!

1 can artichoke hearts, drained
½ teaspoon Worcestershire sauce
1 cup good quality mayonnaise
1 cup Parmesan cheese, grated
2 tablespoons onions, finely minced
Garnish: Paprika

1. Preheat oven to 350 degrees.
2. Place all ingredients in food processor and blend thoroughly.
3. Spoon into 4-cup baking dish and sprinkle top with paprika. Bake 15 to 20 minutes.   Serve with melba toast or toasted Pita Triangles (see Index).

Serves 12.

Wer nach China reisen will,
Muss den ersten Schritt tun.

Artichoke Balls

This was one of my first recipes as a young bride. They have always been a hit at our parties. Be sure you make enough because they disappear fast.

1 8-ounce jar marinated artichoke hearts and liquid
¾ cup fresh mushrooms, sliced
2 garlic cloves
2 cups Parmesan cheese, grated
1½ cups dry bread crumbs
2 eggs
1 teaspoon Jane's Crazy Mixed-up Salt or ½ teaspoon each of salt and pepper

1. Preheat oven to 375 degrees.
2. Using a food processor, finely chop artichoke hearts (with the liquid), mushrooms and garlic.
3. Transfer artichoke mixture to a mixing bowl. Add cheese, 1 cup bread crumbs, eggs, salt and pepper. Mix well.
4. Form into small balls, using a rounded teaspoon and roll in remaining bread crumbs.
5. Bake on greased cookie sheet for 20 minutes. Serve hot.

Serves 24 to 30.

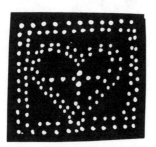

If you want to go to China you have to take the first step

Deviled Eggs

Tina prepared this dish for our family gatherings on Easter Sundays. We developed this recipe together when she was a little girl just beginning to learn how to cook. The eggs are pretty arranged on a platter and nestled in a bed of fresh dill.

12 eggs, hard boiled
2 tablespoons mayonnaise
2 tablespoons Miracle Whip
2 tablespoons sweet pickle relish
1 teaspoon curry powder
2 teaspoons fresh dill or 1 teaspoon dried dill
Pepper to taste, freshly ground
Garnish: Paprika

1. Slice the peeled eggs in half and combine the egg yolks in a small bowl.

2. Add the mayonnaise, Miracle Whip, sweet pickle relish, curry powder, dill, and the pepper to the egg yolks and mix with a fork.

3. Mound a spoonful of the mixture into the white part of the egg and sprinkle with paprika to garnish.

Viele Tropfen machen einen Eimer voll.

Summer Pepper Cheese Ball

For snacks or party time, this is easy to prepare - and it's light and refreshing!

1 8-ounce package cream cheese*
1 tablespoon dry white wine
2 garlic cloves, crushed
2 tablespoons fresh herbs, finely minced (parsley, basil, dill,
oregano or chives - or any combination of your choosing)
1 to 2 tablespoons pepper, freshly ground

Note: For another good variation, use 4 ounces cream cheese and 4
ounces goat cheese.

    1. Measure all ingredients into food processor. Process until cheese
is creamy and all ingredients are well blended.
    2. Form into a ball or place in a crock. Coat with crushed pepper.
Wrap or cover with plastic wrap and chill for several hours until firm.

Serves 8.

Many drops fill one bucket.

Arugula Pesto Torta

For large parties, increase the recipe as needed, and mold into wonderful heart or oval shapes. Garnish with nasturtium flowers or pansies.

1 cup goat cheese
1 recipe Arugula Pesto (see Index)
3 tablespoons pine nuts, lightly toasted

1. Using half of the goat cheese, form into a nice round shape.
2. Spread half of the pesto and one tablespoon of the pine nuts over the goat cheese.
3. Layer the remaining half of the goat cheese over the pesto.
4. Spread the remaining pesto over the goat cheese.
5. Sprinkle with remaining pine nuts. Serve with slices of French bread or crackers.

Serves 4.

New Year's Black-eyed Pea Spread

This great spread is a New Year's tradition in my friend Sally Layne's family but don't limit it to once a year - it's really delicious and should be enjoyed often!

2 15-ounce cans black-eyed peas, drained
1½ cups Monterey Jack cheese with jalapeños, shredded
½ cup green onion, chopped
½ small onion, chopped
1 garlic clove, minced
½ cup butter
1 4-ounce can green chiles, drained

1. Preheat oven to 350 degrees.
2. Blend all ingredients in food processor just until mixed.
3. Pour into greased baking dish and bake for 20 minutes or until hot. Serve hot or cold with chips or vegetables.

Makes 3 to 4 cups.

Roasted Garlic

I think this is one of the most exciting appetizers. Roasting the garlic gives it a mild sweet flavor - the texture becomes like soft butter - making it easy to spread on slices of Tuscan Bread (see Index). I like to arrange the bread on a pretty cutting board, add a wedge of Brie, the Roasted Garlic, and Tomatillo Salsa (see Index). I sure hope there's plenty of garlic in heaven!!

4 to 6 garlic pods
1 tablespoon olive oil
Rosemary sprigs, optional

1. Preheat oven to 350 degrees.
2. Remove loose outer peeling of garlic pods. Slice the tips of each clove so the flesh is exposed.
3. Place on sheet of parchment paper. Drizzle olive oil over top of each garlic pod. Place rosemary with garlic on parchment.
4. Fold parchment around garlic and tuck in ends.
5. Bake for 1 hour. Let cool for 15 minutes before opening parchment.

Note: Garlic can be removed from the skin and kept in the freezer, ready to use in cooking. Roasted garlic has a unique flavor and enhances many recipes, such as Roasted Garlic Mayo (see Index).

Liebe macht blind.

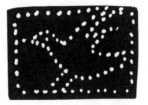

Love is blind.

Brie in Brioche

Peggy Cox is my dear friend who has the same passion for cooking and food preparation that I do. We have enjoyed catering and entertaining together long before she came to manage the Tea Room for me.

Peggy is well known in Fredericksburg for her dramatic presentations of Brie baked in a crusty brioche. I learned the technique from Peggy, and it is a show stopper. Look for the one I did in the picture next to my Mother's St. Francis, and be inspired to do your own. Have fun creating your own decorations on top with the dough scraps!

1 2-kilo Brie or two 1-kilo Bries
Brioche Dough, risen and chilled (recipe follows)
Egg glaze (1 egg beaten with 1 teaspoon water)

Brioche Dough:
    1 tablespoon yeast
    ¼ cup warm water
    ¼ pound butter
    ¼ cup milk
    3½ cups unbleached wheat flour
    2 teaspoons salt
    4 teaspoons sugar
    4 large eggs

    1. Dissolve yeast in warm water. Set aside. In small saucepan over low heat, melt butter in milk.
    2. In a large bowl, combine flour, salt, sugar, eggs, dissolved yeast and milk-butter mixture. Beat with wooden spoon for about 3 minutes. (This step can also be done in a food processor using a plastic blade.) Place dough in an oiled bowl and cover with towel. Let rise until doubled.
    3. Punch dough down into bowl and cover with plastic wrap. Place in refrigerator for 4 to 6 hours or overnight.

Assembling the Brie and Brioche:
    1. Preheat oven to 400 degrees.
    2. Remove brioche dough from fridge, turn onto lightly floured surface. Roll out into a circle with rolling pin, ⅛" thick.
    3. Place Brie carefully on dough - bring up dough to cover the entire surface of the Brie. Where the dough overlaps itself, cut away the excess.

4. Carefully turn the Brie in Brioche over so the smooth side is up. Brush top with egg glaze. Cut out pretty decorative shapes with excess dough. Carefully place decorations on glazed surface of dough - the shapes will adhere so it's important to work quickly and have your design worked out before you begin. Brush with glaze again.

5. Place in oven immediately, before the dough rises.

6. Bake for 30 to 45 minutes until crust is puffed and golden.

7. Remove from oven and let rest at least 30 minutes before serving.

Serves 24.

Hummus

Hummus is best if it's made several hours ahead so the flavors can blend. Serve with toasted Pita Bread Triangles (see Index). This also makes a great "good for you" sandwich filling with lettuce and tomato, and Roasted Garlic Mayo (see Index).

6 garlic cloves, crushed
3 cups cooked garbanzo beans plus ½ cup liquid
¼ cup tahini*
¼ cup freshly squeezed lemon juice
4 tablespoons olive oil
¼ cup fresh parsley, chopped
1 teaspoon pepper, freshly ground

1. Using a food processor, chop garlic until finely minced.

2. Add garbanzos, tahini, lemon juice, and olive oil. Process until all ingredients are coarsely chopped and mixed thoroughly.

3. Stir in parsley and pepper.

Serves 24 to 30 as an appetizer.

*Note: Tahini is a paste made from ground sesame seeds and is available in specialty or natural food stores.

Viele Koche verderben den Brei.

Too many cooks are spoiling the broth

Tomatillo Salsa

We enjoy this salsa, especially when black beans are included in the menu. It's delicious as an appetizer with tortilla chips and also is especially good as a garnish for grilled chicken or beef.

3 garlic cloves, minced
½ to 1 small onion, chopped
1 pound tomatillos, quartered
1 jalapeño
2 tablespoons lime juice
½ cup fresh cilantro, chopped
1 teaspoon salt
1 teaspoon pepper, freshly ground
Salt to taste

1. Place garlic in food processor and mince well. Add onion and pulse to chop.

2. Add remaining ingredients and process until all ingredients are chopped and blended. Don't over process. I like to keep this one rather chunky.

3. Refrigerate for several hours before serving so the flavors can blend. It's delicious when served with fresh toasted corn tortilla chips.

Makes 3 cups.

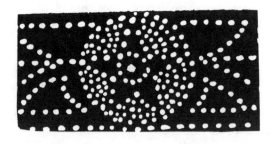

En dónde hay gordura hay hermosura.

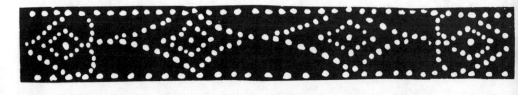

Guacamole

We developed this recipe to serve in our Tea Room. The addition of lime juice and cilantro enhances the flavor. A great topping for chalupas or tacos.

6 to 8 avocados, peeled and seeded
1 tablespoon lemon or lime juice
2 to 4 tablespoons jalapeños, coarsely chopped
¼ cup picante salsa
½ cup cilantro, chopped
1 tablespoon garlic, finely minced
4 tablespoons onion, finely chopped
½ teaspoon salt
½ teaspoon pepper

1. Mash avocado with potato masher to desired consistency. (I like mine chunky, not too smooth.)
2. Stir in remaining ingredients and mix thoroughly. Taste for salt and add more if desired.

Makes 4 to 6 cups.

Peanut Butter Stuffed Jalapeños

Don't pass this recipe by - you will be delightfully surprised at what a treat these are! Include them with your next Mexican buffet. Those who like them...really like them!

1 12-ounce can mild pickled jalapeños
1¼ cups chunky peanut butter
Garnish: Cilantro sprigs

1. Remove jalapeños from can and drain. Slice jalapeños in half lengthwise and remove seeds.
2. Place 1 tablespoon peanut butter in each half. Arrange on serving platter. Garnish with fresh cilantro sprigs.

Serves 6.

Where there is fatness, there is beauty.

Frijole Mole

A colorful dip served with tortilla chips. Delicioso!

4 garlic cloves, minced
1 medium onion, chopped
3 tablespoons pickled jalapeños, chopped
⅓ cup fresh oregano
2 pounds tomatoes, coarsely chopped
½ cup cider vinegar
2 cups corn
2 cups black beans, cooked
Salt and pepper to taste

1. Mince garlic in food processor. Add onion, jalapeños, oregano, and chop coarsely. Place ingredients in mixing bowl.

2. Place tomatoes in food processor and chop coarsely. Add to ingredients in mixing bowl.

3. Stir in remaining ingredients. Taste for salt and pepper.

4. Place in refrigerator for several hours before serving. Serve with fresh, toasted corn tortilla chips.

Makes 8 cups.

Si no te queres quemar, salte de la cocina.

Arugula Pesto Torta and
Tuscan Bread

Cilindritos

"It has been said that cilindrito making is an art learned by apprenticeship and practiced according to intuition. This refers to the forming of the cream cheese around the jalapeño strips, the only difficult part of making cilindritos. I'll do my best to describe it, but plan to experiment for a while the first time you make these before you get the knack." - Ottis Layne

> *(Ottis, another good friend, is an emergency room physician - he occasionally moonlights as a cilindrito cook when our families gather for an evening of good food and fellowship).*

1 8-ounce package cream cheese
1 8-ounce can pickled jalapeños, cut in quarters lengthwise
(remove seeds)
Vegetable oil
1 cup flour
1 cup buttermilk
2 cups corn meal

1. Place the block of cream cheese on the long edge. Using a wire cheese cutter, slice into approximately 20 strips, about ¼" thick.

2. Assemble each cilindrito by stacking the two strips of jalapeño on one slice of cream cheese and putting another slice of cream cheese on top (like a sandwich). Mold the cream cheese around the jalapeño strips, working the edges together and sealing the ends until the jalapeño strips are entirely surrounded by cream cheese.

3. Preheat oil in a skillet, deep enough to almost cover the cilindritos. The oil should be hot enough to fry the cilindritos fast.

4. Roll each cilindrito in flour, dip in buttermilk, and roll in corn meal. Fry them until light brown, turn as needed.

Makes 10 to 12 cilindritos.

If you do not want to get burned, get out of the kitchen.

Queso de Oaxaca

Serve these with Peach Margaritas (see following page) - a great party opener!

6 poblano chilies, roasted and peeled
1 onion, halved and cut in strips
2 to 3 tablespoons vegetable oil
8 ounces cream cheese, cut in 4 to 5 pieces
½ teaspoon garlic powder
Pinch of cumin
Salt to taste
6 ounces Oaxaca or mozzarella cheese, grated
6 to 8 hot flour tortillas

1. Stem and seed chilies and cut into narrow strips.
2. Sauté onion in oil until soft and translucent, about 5 to 8 minutes. Do not brown.
3. Add chilies and cook 1 minute, then add the cream cheese and spices. When the cream cheese is completely melted, add the grated Oaxaca or mozzarella in 6 to 8 handfuls. Allow the cheese to melt without stirring and take care to keep the temperature low.
4. Place in individual ramekins with a hot flour tortilla draped over the top of each bowl. To eat, spoon mixture onto the tortilla, roll or fold to keep the mixture from spilling out.

Note: The chile and onion mixture may be prepared up to 2 days in advance and either refrigerated or frozen until ready to use. Be sure to reheat it before adding the 2 cheeses.

Serves 6 to 8.

Las penas con pan son menos.

Hardships are less painful on a full stomach.

Frozen Peach Margaritas

Margarita fans, you're going to love these! They are always a hit at summer parties. Make them ahead of time, keep them in the freezer, ready to serve to your guests as they arrive.

1 6-ounce can frozen limeade
6 ounces tequila
6 ounces Triple Sec
6 tablespoons lime juice
2 cups fresh peaches
4 cups ice cubes

1. Combine all ingredients except ice in blender. Blend well.
2. Pour half of the mixture into a container. Then add 2 cups ice to the mixture in the blender and blend well. Pour the blended margarita into a container for the freezer.
3. Pour the remaining half of the mixture into the blender and add 2 cups ice to blend. Place in the freezer until ready to serve.

Serves 6 to 8.

Note: Fresh peaches are a must. Put a supply of peaches in your freezer to enjoy throughout the year!

Lemonade

I love to keep this in our fridge in the summertime. I like it because it's not too sweet. Garnish with a sprig of fresh mint or lemon balm and lemon slices.

1½ cups fresh lemon juice - use only fresh juice, not bottled
¾ cup maple syrup
7 cups water
Garnish: Fresh mint or lemon balm and lemon slices.

1. Mix well and chill.
2. Serve over ice cubes and garnish.

Serves 8.

Carlos' Eggnog

Store-bought doesn't compare to this easy-to-make eggnog. Carlos keeps this recipe in his wallet - handy for when he comes home for the holidays. He makes this for our family every Christmas Eve - a tradition we all enjoy.

6 eggs, separated
¾ cup sugar
2 cups heavy whipping cream
1 cup milk
1 cup half and half
1 cup brandy or whiskey
Nutmeg

1. Chill liquids before mixing. Beat yolks and add sugar.
2. In a separate bowl, whip the heavy whipping cream until soft peaks form.
3. Fold the whipped cream into the milk, half and half, and brandy or whiskey. Add yolks and sugar. Beat egg whites and fold in. Add nutmeg and chill.

Serves 6.

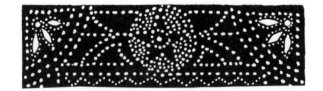

La gloria y el infierno están aquí en la tierra.

Heaven and Hell are here on earth.

Soups

Asparagus Soup

What a delicious way to celebrate spring!

3 garlic cloves, minced
1 medium onion, chopped
3 tablespoons butter
1 pound asparagus, cut in 1" lengths
⅓ cup flour
1 teaspoon pepper
6 cups chicken broth
2 cups milk or light cream
1 tablespoon lemon juice
Salt to taste

1. Sauté garlic and onion in butter until very soft. Stir in asparagus and cook for 2 or 3 minutes until asparagus turns bright green.

2. Add flour and stir until asparagus is well coated. Add pepper and chicken broth. Bring to a boil quickly. Boil for 1 minute, add milk or cream. Turn off heat. Add lemon juice. Test for salt and pepper. Serve immediately.

Serves 6.

Nach getaner Arbeit ist's gut ruh'n.

Asparagus-Mushroom-Potato Soup

The combination of these ingredients makes for a delightful soup - substantial but not heavy - great for a light spring supper.

1 leek, sliced
3 cups mushrooms, sliced
3 tablespoons butter
3 garlic cloves, minced
6 cups red potatoes, cubed - unpeeled
10 cups chicken broth
1½ teaspoons pepper, freshly ground
1 pound asparagus, sliced into 1½" lengths
Salt to taste
Garnish: Sour cream or Crème Fraîche (see Index)

1. In a stock pot, sauté the leeks and mushrooms in the butter and garlic until they are tender.
2. Add the potatoes, chicken broth and pepper and cook until the potatoes are soft. The asparagus should be added last and cooked only until crisp tender - about 5 to 10 minutes. Salt to taste. Garnish with a dollop of sour cream or Crème Fraîche.

Serves 10 to 12.

Do your work first then rest.

Celeriac Soup

In the springtime, go to your specialty grocery store and look for celery root, or celeriac. It's very good sliced into salads and makes a delicious soup - really special because its seasonal.

1 leek, chopped
2 tablespoons butter
1 tablespoon garlic, roasted or 3 garlic cloves, minced
1 celeriac root, peeled and cubed (about 3 cups)
2 to 3 medium potatoes, peeled and cubed (about 3 cups)
5 cups chicken broth
1 teaspoon pepper
1 cup evaporated milk
Salt to taste
Garnish: Fresh chives and Crème Fraîche (see Index)

1. Sauté leek and butter. Add garlic, sauté 1 more minute.
2. Add celeriac, potatoes, chicken broth, pepper and cook until potatoes and celeriac root are soft, about 30 to 40 minutes. Add milk. Taste for salt. Garnish with fresh chives and Crème Fraîche.

Serves 8 to 10.

Arbeit macht das Leben suss, Faulheit
starkt die Glieder.

Potato and Green Garlic Soup

I've recently discovered many uses for green garlic. It has a very short season, so you have to be on the lookout for it in the springtime. This soup is one of the ways we enjoy it at home and in the Tea Room.

> **3 pounds medium potatoes**
> **6 cups green garlic, chopped**
> **6 tablespoons butter**
> **6 to 8 cups water or chicken broth**
> **1 cup half and half or evaporated milk**
> **Salt and pepper to taste**
> **Garnish: Sour cream**

1. Peel and cube potatoes. Wash, trim, and chop the green garlic using as much of the green top as is fresh.
2. In a large stock pot, melt butter and add green garlic. Cook lightly on medium heat until wilted.
3. Add potatoes and broth. Bring to a boil, reduce heat and simmer until potatoes are tender, about 40 to 45 minutes. If a thicker soup is desired, drain some of the liquid at this time.
4. Add half and half or evaporated milk and heat before serving.
5. Salt and pepper to taste. Garnish with sour cream.

Serves 14 to 16.

Potato-Green Garlic-Jalapeño Soup

Same as above, add ¼ to ½ cup sliced pickled jalapeños with potatoes and broth.

Note: Green garlic is garlic that is harvested before the garlic bulb forms and develops. It is milder than the garlic cloves we are accustomed to using. The entire bulb and stalk can be used. It is delicious when braised and served with lamb in the springtime.

To work sweetens one's life, but to be lazy makes you strong.

Kale and Potato Soup

My dear friend, Dr. Charles Schmidt, is well known for the wonderful buffets he creates for several community benefits in Fredericksburg. Being the good frugal German he is, he carefully rescues the kale from the serving platters when the party is over and freezes it for making this delicious soup.

4 medium potatoes, chopped
2 tablespoons vegetable oil
8 cups water
1 teaspoon salt
½ teaspoon pepper
2 pounds fresh kale, thinly shredded
½ pound cooked, smoked garlic sausage, sliced

1. Combine potatoes with vegetable oil and water. Cook for 20 to 30 minutes or until potatoes are tender.

2. Remove potatoes and reserve liquid. Mash potatoes through a sieve and return to potato liquid. Add salt and pepper and simmer for 20 minutes.

3. Add kale to potatoes and cook for 25 minutes.

4. Add sausage. Simmer gently for 5 minutes. Serve.

Serves 6 to 8.

Alt wie eine Kuh und man lernt immer noch dazu.

Texas 1015 Onion Soup

This soup is dedicated to our good friend, Bob Gates - who loves onions anyway I prepare them!

¼ cup butter
3 to 4 large Texas Sweet Onions (8 cups), sliced
3 tablespoons sugar
1 cup white wine
8 cups chicken broth
1 teaspoon salt
2 teaspoons pepper
2 cups milk
⅛ teaspoon soda (to prevent curdling)
Garnish: Chopped chives and chive blossoms, if available.

1. Melt butter in stock pot.
2. Add onions and cook slowly until wilted and soft.
3. Sprinkle sugar over onions. Cover surface of onions with piece of waxed paper while cooking over low heat for 45 minutes until onions are caramelized (golden).
4. Add wine, chicken broth, salt, pepper and cook covered over medium heat for 15 minutes. Add milk and soda. Heat thoroughly and serve.

Serves 10 to 12.

Old as a cow and still learning.

Fancy Mushroom-Wild Rice Soup

This is a very elegant soup. For special occasions, gather a bouquet of about five Enochi mushrooms and tie them together with a garlic chive - float one on top of each serving - very impressive!

¼ cup butter
1 large leek, sliced (3 cups)
½ cup rice*
3 to 4 garlic cloves, minced
4 to 6 cups mushrooms (use combination of Shitake,
Portabella, etc., whatever you find that looks interesting!)
10 cups chicken or beef broth
½ teaspoon pepper, freshly ground
½ cup evaporated milk
½ cup white wine, optional
Salt to taste
Garnish: ½ cup Enochi mushrooms, garlic chives and Crème
Fraîche (see Index)

1. Melt butter in large saucepan. Add leeks and rice, and sauté until leeks are soft and rice is golden. The flavor is greatly improved when you follow this step.
2. Add garlic and mushrooms. Continue to cook, stirring 3 to 4 minutes.
3. Add broth and pepper. Bring to a boil and simmer, covered for 40 minutes, or until rice is tender.
4. Add evaporated milk, optional white wine and heat thoroughly. Taste for salt. Garnish with Crème Fraîche and a few lightly steamed Enochi mushrooms.

Serves 6 to 8.

Note: This is up to you--brown rice, wild rice, or a mixture of your choosing, maybe half and half. Remember to adjust cooking time depending on the type of rice you choose.

Tuscan Vegetable Soup

Vegetables from Marianne and Steve's organic farm inspired this wonderful soup. The peppers looked so pretty on my kitchen counter that I was tempted to keep them for visual enjoyment - they were red, yellow, golden, pale green and purple. This soup turned out to be one of my favorites! A real taste of Hill Country Provence. If you have some pesto in your freezer, add a spoonful as a garnish when serving!

1 cup white beans
3 garlic cloves, minced
4 cups water
2 tablespoons olive oil
1 leek, chopped (2 cups)
2 carrots, sliced
½ pound Italian sausage
10 cups chicken broth
2 cups red and yellow peppers, sliced
2 teaspoons pepper, freshly ground
1 turnip, sliced
4 cups mustard greens, coarsely chopped
Salt to taste
Garnish: Parmesan or Romano cheese, grated

1. Cook white beans and garlic in water until beans are tender, about 2 hours.

2. Sauté olive oil, leeks, carrots and Italian sausage. Add to beans.

3. Add remaining ingredients. Cook over medium heat for 30 to 45 minutes, until vegetables are tender. Taste for salt and pepper. Garnish with grated Parmesan or Romano cheese.

Serves 12.

Morgen Stund' hat Gold im Mund.

Those who rise early get the gold.

Fiesta Gazpacho

Gazpacho is a great way to enjoy fresh homegrown tomatoes during the summer. I like to keep it in the fridge. It's great to have on hand for light meals or snacks - and it's loaded with vitamins and fiber.

2 garlic cloves
1 medium onion
6 large tomatoes, peeled
2 small cucumbers, peeled, seeded
1 green pepper, seeded
1 red pepper, seeded
2 cups frozen corn
2 cups black beans, cooked
1 46-ounce can tomato juice
2 tablespoons red wine vinegar
2 tablespoons olive oil
1 teaspoon salt
1 teaspoon pepper
¼ teaspoon Tabasco
2 tablespoons pickled jalapeños, seeded
¼ cup fresh oregano
Garnish: Cucumber slices, unpeeled and sprig of fresh oregano

1. In a large food processor, chop garlic and onion and tomatoes. Remove from processor and place in a large bowl.

2. In the processor, coarsely chop peeled and seeded cucumbers and seeded green and red peppers. Then add corn and black beans. It is important that they are not chopped too finely.

3. Add cucumbers and pepper to tomato mixture. Add remaining ingredients and adjust seasonings. You may need to add additional tomato juice as it thickens. Chill thoroughly. This is best made the day before serving. Garnish with unpeeled cucumber slices and a sprig of fresh oregano.

Serves 14 to 16.

El envidioso nunca da un cumplimiento, solamente tra

Tomato-Brown Rice Soup

Browning the rice, and the combination of ingredients, develops the unique flavor found in this soup. This is one of the most requested soups in the Tea Room.

¾ cup brown rice
1 medium onion, chopped
2 to 3 garlic cloves, minced
2 bell peppers, chopped
3 tablespoons olive oil
10 cups chicken broth
6 cups canned tomatoes, crushed
1½ teaspoons thyme
1½ teaspoons marjoram
1½ teaspoons pepper, freshly ground
Salt to taste
Garnish: Fresh parsley, chopped

1. In a large stock pot, lightly brown the rice, onion, garlic and bell peppers in the olive oil.
2. Add the chicken broth, tomatoes, herbs and bring to a boil. Reduce heat and cook for 30 to 40 minutes until rice is tender. Taste for salt and pepper. Garnish with fresh chopped parsley.

Serves 16.

The envious person never compliments, he only swallows.

Sherried Tomato Consommé

As simple as a soup can be - and with great rewards! It's a good choice for a ladies' luncheon when you need extra time for preparing fancy sandwiches and cookies - and flower arranging!

1 46-ounce can tomato juice
2 10½-ounce cans beef bouillon
½ cup sherry
1 tablespoon dried dill
1 tablespoon lemon juice
Garnish: Lemon, thinly sliced

Combine all ingredients in a stock pot. Heat thoroughly. Garnish each serving with a thin lemon slice. It looks pretty floating on top!

Serves 6 to 8.

Sorrel Soup

Sorrel leaves have the appearance of spinach - but their flavor is tart and lemony - look for it in the springtime. Chives and chive blossoms are a pretty garnish for Sorrel Soup and they are usually in season at the same time.

1 medium onion, chopped
2 garlic cloves, minced
¼ cup butter
6 cups chicken broth
3 medium potatoes, cubed
1 teaspoon salt
1 teaspoon pepper
8 cups sorrel, coarsely chopped
1 cup milk
Garnish: Chopped chives and chive blossoms, if available.

1. Sauté onion and garlic in butter.
2. Add chicken broth and potatoes, salt and pepper. Cook until potatoes are tender - about 20 to 30 minutes. Break up potatoes with potato masher.
3. Add sorrel, cook 10 minutes.
4. Add milk. Heat thoroughly.

Serves 8.

Garden Cream of Tomato Soup

Last summer, my good friend Martha Kipcak brought me beautiful ripe tomatoes from her garden and this fabulous recipe. It deserves a Blue Ribbon! I prepare it often in the Tea Room.

¼ cup olive oil
2 tablespoons butter
2 carrots, finely diced
1 green bell peppers, diced
4 stalks celery, finely diced
1 medium onion, minced
4 garlic cloves, minced
10 cups tomatoes, peeled and cut into large pieces
6 cups water
¼ cup fresh parsley, chopped
½ cup fresh basil, chopped
1 tablespoon salt
1 tablespoon pepper
¼ teaspoon baking soda
1½ cups evaporated milk
Garnish: Chives or green onions, finely chopped

1. In a large stock pot, heat olive oil and butter. Add carrots, bell peppers, celery, onions and garlic. Simmer 30 minutes until tender.
2. Add tomatoes and water and continue to cook 30 minutes more.
3. Add parsley and basil, salt and pepper. Measure in the baking soda and evaporated milk. Cook until heated thoroughly. Garnish with freshly snipped chives or finely chopped green onions.

Serves 12 to 14.

Del plato a la boca a veces se cae la sopa
From the plate to the mouth sometimes the soup is spilled.

Chili Poblano

One of Hector's favorite soups! A wonderful soup to have left over so you can use it for an enchilada sauce or to dress up the Bean Cakes (see Index) for a really special appetizer.

2 tablespoons butter
1 medium onion, chopped
2 garlic cloves, minced
2 cups carrots, sliced
¼ cup flour
6 cups chicken broth
1½ cups green chilies, coarsely chopped
¼ to ½ cup cilantro, chopped
¼ teaspoon baking soda
1¼ cups evaporated milk
Salt and pepper to taste
Garnish: Sour cream and almonds, toasted

1. Melt butter in a stock pot. Sauté onions, garlic, and carrots. Add flour and cook for 5 minutes.

2. Stir in the chicken broth, green chilies, and cilantro. Mix thoroughly and simmer for 30 minutes.

3. Strain vegetables in colander, reserving juice. Purée the vegetables in food processor until smooth and return them with the reserved juice to the sauce pan.

4. Add baking soda and then the evaporated milk. Heat thoroughly. Taste for salt and pepper. Garnish with sour cream and toasted almonds.

Serves 10.

Cuando no hay lomo de todo como.

Harvest Bisque

Peggy Cox's wonderful soup is great for the fall season. It has a very rich flavor and texture. It's hard to believe that this rich soup is so good for you - only 120 calories per cup!

1 (2-pound) butternut squash
2 tablespoons olive oil
2 cups leeks, chopped
1 cup red pepper, coarsely chopped
6 cups chicken broth
3 cups carrot, diced
3 cups potato, cubed
1 tablespoon fresh parsley, chopped
1 teaspoon fresh thyme, chopped
¼ to ½ teaspoon pepper
½ cup skim milk
Garnish: Fresh chives

1. Cut squash in half lengthwise; place squash, cut side down, in microwave dish. Cover with plastic wrap and microwave on high until soft (about 12 minutes). Let cool to touch. Remove and discard seeds. Scoop out and reserve pulp; discard shells.

2. In a large stock pot, add oil and sauté leeks and red pepper until just tender. Stir in broth and remaining ingredients except milk. Bring to a boil; cover, reduce heat, and simmer 20 to 25 minutes or until vegetables are tender.

3. Process reserved squash pulp and 2 cups vegetable mixture; process until smooth. Add vegetable purée to remaining vegetable mixture. Stir in milk. Cook over medium-low heat until thoroughly heated. Garnish with chives.

Serves 10.

When there is no beef to eat, I will eat of what there is.

Corn and Potato Chowder

A delicious and comforting soup - good anytime!

¼ pound bacon
1 medium onion, chopped
2 garlic cloves, minced
2 cups potatoes, cubed
6 cups water
½ cup pimentos, sliced
1 teaspoon dried thyme
5 cups corn, chopped in food processor
1½ cups evaporated milk
½ cup fresh parsley, chopped
2 teaspoons salt
1 teaspoon pepper, freshly ground
Garnish: Fresh parsley sprigs

1. In a stock pot, sauté bacon until light brown. Add onions, garlic and cook until soft.

2. Add potatoes, water, pimentos and thyme. Cook until potatoes are tender. Add corn and cook for about 10 minutes. Add milk, - parsley, salt, pepper and heat thoroughly. Garnish with fresh parsley sprig.

Serves 8.

**Bier und Wein, das lass sein.
Wein und Bier, das rat' ich Dir.**

Corn Cheddar Chowder

This is a delicious soup that I've made in the Tea Room since we opened 10 years ago and accidently did not include in my first cookbook. Notice that it's totally meat-free! The unique flavor comes from the wonderful mix of ingredients.

1 onion, chopped
3 to 4 garlic cloves, minced
¼ cup butter
12 cups water
½ cup dry white wine
6 medium potatoes, peeled and cubed
2 teaspoons thyme, dried
1 tablespoon ground comino
1 teaspoon sage
2 teaspoon pepper, freshly ground
2 bay leaves
3 to 4 teaspoons salt
4 cups frozen corn
2 cups evaporated milk
2 cups Cheddar cheese, grated
¼ teaspoon nutmeg
3 tablespoons fresh parsley, chopped
Garnish: Cheddar cheese, grated, and parsley sprig.

1. In a large stock pot, sauté onions and garlic in butter.
2. Add the water, wine, potatoes, thyme, comino, sage, pepper, bay leaves, and salt. Cook until the potatoes are done.
3. Add corn, milk, and cheese and continue to cook about 10 to 15 minutes until corn is tender.
4. Add the nutmeg and parsley just before serving. Garnish with Cheddar cheese and a parsley sprig.

Serves 16 to 18.

Beer on top of wine is no good. But wine over beer is fine.

Butternut Squash Soup

Be sure to try this soup. The ingredients are nutritious and if you use skim milk, it's almost fat free! The pumpkin seeds are a terrific taste complement.

1 leek, chopped, (3 cups)
2 garlic cloves, minced
1 tablespoon butter
1 tablespoon olive oil
1 butternut squash (about 3 pounds), peeled and cut into 2" cubes
6 to 8 cups chicken broth
½ green apple, unpeeled, diced
1 teaspoon salt
½ teaspoon pepper
¼ teaspoon nutmeg
1 cup evaporated milk or cream
Garnish: Pumpkin seeds, lightly toasted and chopped, and thinned sour cream or yogurt

1. In a stock pot, sauté leek and garlic in butter and olive oil until soft.
2. Add squash, chicken broth, apple, salt, and pepper. Heat to boiling and cook for 15 to 20 minutes until squash is very soft.
3. Place half of the squash mixture into food processor. Process until smooth, being very careful, as hot liquid will expand. Repeat with remaining squash mixture.
4. Transfer back into the stock pot. Add nutmeg and milk and stir to combine. Taste for salt and pepper. Heat and serve. Garnish with a swirl of thinned sour cream or yogurt and toasted pumpkin seeds.

Serves 10 to 12.

Una boca cerrado no pesca moscas.

Calabacitas Soup

This squash soup was inspired by the vegetable dish Hector's mother used to make. The flavors are the same, but now it's the main event!

4 slices bacon, diced
1 large onion, chopped
3 garlic cloves, minced
8 large yellow squash, sliced
2 large zucchini squash, sliced
10 cups chicken broth
½ cup green chilies, chopped
½ cup pimentos, chopped
5 teaspoons ground comino
2 teaspoons oregano
16 ounces frozen corn (or 2 cups)
¼ teaspoon baking soda
2 to 4 cups evaporated milk
Salt to taste
2 teaspoons pepper
Garnish: Monterey Jack cheese, shredded, and green onions, chopped.

1. In a large stock pot, sauté bacon, onion and garlic.
2. Add yellow squash, zucchini, chicken broth, chilies, pimentos, comino and oregano. Bring to a boil. Then cook until squash is almost tender.
3. Add corn. Simmer about 10 minutes.
4. Add baking soda and evaporated milk and heat thoroughly. Taste for salt and pepper. Garnish with Monterey Jack cheese and green onions.

Serves 16 to 18 cups.

A closed mouth catches no flies.

Chicken and Barley Soup

A nutritious low fat soup, very flavorful - the barley provides lots of B vitamins!

1 medium onion, chopped
2 garlic cloves, minced
6 carrots (4 cups), cleaned and sliced
2 ribs celery (1 cup), sliced
4 tablespoons butter
12 cups chicken broth
½ teaspoon thyme
½ teaspoon pepper
1 cup pearl barley
1 bay leaf
½ teaspoon ground comino
½ teaspoon nutmeg
4 cups chicken, cooked and cubed
Salt to taste
4 tablespoons fresh parsley, finely chopped
Garnish: Fresh parsley, chopped

1. In a large stock pot, sauté the onions, garlic, carrots, and celery in the butter.

2. Add the chicken broth, thyme, pepper, barley, bay leaf, comino, and nutmeg. Bring the soup to a simmer and cook until the barley is tender, about 45 to 50 minutes.

3. Add the chicken and simmer gently for 5 more minutes, stirring occasionally. Taste for salt and pepper. Add the parsley last and serve. Garnish with chopped fresh parsley.

Serves 16.

Ich bin klein, mein Herz ist rein. soll
neimand drin wohnen als Gott allein.

Monterey Chicken Soup

Our customers really love this soup - it's a good choice any time of the year, especially when we have cool weather.

3 tablespoon olive oil
1½ medium onions, chopped
2 large garlic cloves, minced
3 4-ounce cans green chilies, diced
3 teaspoons chili powder
3 teaspoons ground comino
3 teaspoons dried oregano, crumbled
12 cups chicken broth, homemade or canned
3 14½-ounce cans tomatoes, diced with juice
4 cups chicken, cubed
4 cups frozen corn, thawed
⅔ cup cilantro, chopped
Salt and pepper to taste
3 cups Monterey Jack cheese, shredded
Corn tortilla triangles, cut into wedges and fried until crisp
Garnish: Green onions, chopped.

1. Heat oil in stock pot over medium-low heat.
2. Add onion and garlic. Sauté until soft. Add chilies, chili powder, comino and oregano. Stir one minute.
3. Mix in broth and tomatoes and their juice. Bring mixture just to a boil. Add chicken, corn, cilantro and simmer until cooked thoroughly, about 15 minutes.
4. Season with salt and pepper.
5. Sprinkle each serving with cheese and corn tortilla triangles. Garnish with green onions.

Serves 16 to 18.

I am small. My heart is pure. May only the spirit of God dwell there in.

Vegetable Chicken Soup

Remember to do this soup in the summertime, when fresh tomatoes, zucchini, and basil are plentiful!

1 onion, chopped
2 or 3 garlic cloves, minced
2 tablespoons olive oil
6 to 8 cups chicken broth or water
4 cups fresh tomatoes, coarsely chopped
½ cup green chilies
2 cups chicken, cooked and cubed
2 tablespoons basil
2 teaspoons pepper, freshly ground
1 large zucchini, sliced
2 cups frozen corn
Salt to taste
Garnish: Grated Romano cheese and fresh parsley

1. Sauté onions and garlic in olive oil.
2. Add broth, tomatoes, chilies, chicken, basil, pepper and bring to a boil. Simmer for 15 minutes.
3. Add zucchini and corn. Cook for about 20 minutes until the zucchini is tender. Taste for salt and pepper. Garnish with grated Romano cheese and parsley.

Serves 10.

Die besten Menchen auf der Erde sind die Hunde und die Pferde.

Tomatillo Chicken Soup

Tomatillos are small green tomatoes native to Mexico - you'll find them in the produce department of large grocery stores. They have a papery brown husk that you remove before washing. All ingredients in this soup combine well to make a flavorful light entrée.

1 medium onion, chopped
3 to 4 garlic cloves, minced
1 cup brown rice
3 tablespoons olive oil
8 cups tomatillos
2 cups green chilies
12 cups chicken broth
4 cups chicken, cooked and cubed
¼ cup cilantro, chopped
2 teaspoons ground comino
Salt to taste
2 teaspoons pepper
Garnish: Sour cream and fresh cilantro sprigs

1. In a stock pot, sauté onions, garlic and brown rice in the olive oil until onions are soft and the rice is golden.
2. Place tomatillos in boiling salted water for about 3 minutes. Drain and discard cooking water.
3. Place tomatillos and chilies in food processor. Pulse several times to chop coarsely.
4. Add tomatillos and chilies to onion-rice mixture. Add remaining ingredients. Taste for salt and pepper. Cook for about 15 to 20 minutes until rice is done. Garnish with a dollop of sour cream and a sprig of cilantro.

Serves 20.

The best people on the earth are dogs and horses.

Black-eyed Pea and Ham Soup

Serving black-eyed peas and ham at the New Year is a family tradition. We've turned it into a soup - served in the Tea Room on New Year's Eve and lots of other times, too!

1 medium onion, chopped
4 bacon slices, diced
2 teaspoons garlic, minced
1 green bell pepper, chopped
16 cups water
2 10-ounce cans Rotel tomatoes
1 teaspoon pepper, freshly ground
1 pound dried black-eyed peas, sorted and rinsed
2 teaspoons salt
6 carrots, peeled and sliced
2 cups ham, cooked and diced
Garnish: Fresh parsley, chopped

1. In a large stock pot, sauté the onions, bacon, and garlic. Add the bell pepper, water, Rotel tomatoes, pepper, black-eyed peas, salt and carrots. Cook until the peas are tender.

2. Add the ham and cook for about 15 to 20 minutes until carrots are tender. Garnish soup with the freshly chopped parsley.

Serves 16.

Gluck und Glas,
wie leicht bricht das.

White Bean and Ham Soup

The first soup I learned how to make as a child -- my Aunt Jo taught me to make it on one of her visits from Michigan. Plain and simple ingredients - a delicious soup!

2 cups onion, chopped
¼ cup butter or margarine
3 garlic cloves, minced
2 cups carrots, sliced
2 cups celery, sliced
4 cups dried white beans, sorted and rinsed
16 cups chicken broth
2 cups ham, cubed
2 bay leaves
Salt to taste
2 teaspoons pepper
Garnish: Fresh parsley, chopped

1. In a large stock pot, sauté onion in butter or margarine. Add garlic, carrots, and celery and continue cooking for a few minutes.

2. Add the remaining ingredients and bring to a boil. Reduce heat and simmer covered, for 2 hours until beans are very soft. Add more liquid as necessary. Taste for salt and pepper. Garnish with fresh parsley, chopped.

Serves 18 to 20.

Luck and glass, how easy it breaks.

Red Beans and Rice Soup

A very tasty soup. The beans and rice together provide a complete protein meal, plus it's low fat.

1 medium onion, chopped
2 to 3 garlic cloves, minced
3 tablespoons olive oil
4 carrots, sliced
4 celery ribs, sliced
1 green bell pepper, chopped
12 cups water or chicken broth
2 cups red beans, sorted, washed and soaked overnight
1 teaspoon salt
1 teaspoon pepper, freshly ground
1½ teaspoons thyme
1½ teaspoons marjoram
1 14½-ounce can tomatoes with juice, chopped
1 tablespoon jalapeños, chopped
¾ cup brown rice
2 cups ham, cubed
Garnish: Green onions, finely chopped

1. In a large stock pot, sauté onion and garlic in olive oil. Add carrots, celery, and bell pepper and continue sautéing for a few minutes.
2. Add the remaining ingredients except the brown rice and ham and cook covered until beans begin to get tender, about 1½ to 2 hours.
3. Add rice and ham and more liquid, if necessary. Continue cooking until beans are very tender and rice is done. Taste for salt and pepper. Garnish with chopped green onion.

Serves 20.

Heute rot, morgen tot.

Ham and Corn Chowder

Hearty and good. Just a good soup to serve anytime.

1 medium onion, chopped
¼ cup butter
½ cup flour
8 cups chicken broth
3 medium red potatoes, peeled, cubed, and cooked
1 teaspoon pepper, freshly ground
3 cups ham, cubed
6 cups frozen corn
2 cups evaporated milk
Salt to taste
Garnish: Paprika and fresh parsley, chopped

1. In a large stock pot, sauté the onion in butter until tender. Add the flour to make a roux.

2. Pour in the chicken broth and add the potatoes and pepper. Let soup simmer about 30 minutes or until potatoes are tender, stirring occasionally.

3. Add the ham and corn. Simmer 10 more minutes until the soup is heated thoroughly. Add milk. Salt to taste. Garnish with paprika and a parsley sprig.

Serves 16.

Here today, gone tomorrow

Chicken Pozole

Once you've tried this soup you'll be glad it makes a lot. It's good to have some left over. Be sure to include the suggested garnish of avocado and lime. It's really a delicious soup!

½ cup Masa Harina flour
1½ cups cool water
12 cups chicken broth
2 medium garlic cloves, minced
1 medium onion, chopped
1 tablespoon chili powder
1 tablespoon brown sugar
1 tablespoon dried oregano
1 tablespoon ground comino
1 teaspoon pepper, freshly ground
1 cup green chilies, chopped, drained
4 cups chicken pieces
1 30-ounce can white hominy, drained
1 30-ounce can yellow hominy, drained
Salt to taste
Garnish: Lime wedges and avocado slices

1. In a large stock pot, mix Masa Harina flour with the 1½ cup cool water until smooth. Add the chicken broth and bring to a boil.

2. Add the garlic, onion, seasonings and green chilies. Simmer covered for about 15 minutes.

3. Add the chicken and hominy and let it simmer for a while to bring out the flavor. Salt to taste. Garnish with a lime wedge and avocado slice before serving.

Serves 16.

El amor es ciego pero los vecinos no.

Love is blind but not the neighbors.

Chicken Pozole Soup and
Blueberry Pecan Corn
Muffins

Albondigas
(Mexican Meatball Soup)

My mother-in-law taught me to make this soup. It's more like a stew than a soup - very hearty - a recipe I'm sure you will want to repeat often.

2 medium onions, chopped
1 tablespoon garlic, minced
2 tablespoons olive oil
12 cups beef broth or water
4 cups tomatoes, coarsely chopped, with juice
¼ cup cilantro, chopped
1 teaspoon ground comino
2 teaspoons pepper, freshly ground
1 teaspoon salt
¼ cup rice, uncooked
Garnish: Green onions, chopped

1. In a large stock pot, sauté onion and garlic in oil until transparent.

2. Add remaining ingredients, except rice, and bring to a boil. Reduce heat and simmer about 20 minutes. While soup is cooking, make the meatballs.

3. Bring soup to a rolling boil. Drop the meatballs into the boiling soup. Add rice and lower heat to medium for 20 minutes until rice and meatballs are done. Garnish with chopped green onions.

Meatballs:
1 pound ground beef
½ cup rice, uncooked
1 tablespoon ground comino
1 teaspoon salt
1 teaspoon pepper, freshly ground
2 eggs
2 tablespoons flour
½ cup cilantro, finely chopped

1. Mix all ingredients together.
2. Form the meat mixture into tablespoon-size meatballs.

Serves 10 to 12.

Gumbo

Peggy Cox and I collaborated on this recipe for gumbo. Her technique for roux (made in the microwave) is a treasure for your recipe collection. It's so easy - and failproof - and delicious! I particularly like our version because it's a lighter and fresher version of traditional gumbo.

⅔ cup corn oil*
⅔ cup flour
1 green pepper, chopped
2 cups celery, chopped
1 medium onion, chopped
3 to 4 garlic cloves, minced
½ cup fresh parsley
4 cups chicken broth
4 cups water
1 teaspoon pepper
2 cups tomatoes, chopped, with juice
3 chicken breasts, 2" cubes
1 pound smoked sausage, 1" slices
1 cup green onions
1 pound shrimp, peeled and deveined
½ teaspoon gumbo file
¼ teaspoon Tabasco or to taste
Salt to taste
Garnish: Green onions, finely chopped

1. Mix corn oil and flour well and microwave on high for 6 minutes in an 8-cup Pyrex measuring cup. Remove from microwave and stir very well with whisk. Microwave again for 1 minute at a time until roux is a dark walnut brown. Be careful not to let it burn.

2. Add green pepper, celery and onion to roux and microwave on high for 3 minutes. Add garlic and parsley.

Was ich nicht weiss, macht mich nict heiss.

3. Transfer to stock pot and add chicken broth, water, pepper, and tomatoes. Bring to a boil and lower heat and cook for 30 minutes.

4. Add chicken and sausage and cook for 20 minutes.

5. Add green onions, shrimp, gumbo file and Tabasco. Taste for salt and pepper. Cook for another 10 to 15 minutes. Don't overcook at this point so your shrimp will remain tender. Serve in bowls over rice and garnish with green onion.

Serves 10 to 12.

Note: Don't use canola oil, it won't brown.

What you do not know does not bother you.

Autumn Vegetable Soup

It's a hearty soup and makes good use of the vegetables that are plentiful in the fall season. Pork or venison is also a good choice for this soup.

2 tablespoons vegetable oil
2 pounds beef roast, trimmed, cut into 1" cubes
1 large onion, chopped
3 garlic cloves, chopped
10 cups water
2 bay leaves
2 teaspoons dried thyme
2 teaspoons salt
2 teaspoons pepper, freshly ground
1 28-ounce can whole tomatoes, chopped coarsely, with juice
1 large sweet potato, peeled, 1 inch cubes
½ head cauliflower cut into small florets
2 medium turnips, peeled and sliced
½ medium head cabbage, cored and sliced
Garnish: Fresh parsley, finely chopped, or Garlic Croutons
(see index)

1. In a large stock pot, heat oil over medium-high heat. Brown beef well, with onions and garlic.

2. Add water, bay leaves, thyme, salt, and pepper. Cover and heat to boiling. Reduce heat to low, simmer soup 30 minutes until meat is tender.

3. Add tomatoes with their juice to the soup. Stir in sweet potato, cauliflower, turnips, and cabbage; cook until vegetables are tender - about 10 to 15 minutes.

4. Taste for salt and pepper. Add more broth if desired. Garnish with finely chopped parsley or Garlic Croutons.

Serves 18 to 20.

Nadie sabe lo que contiene la olla,

nomás la cuchara que la menea.

Garlic Soup

To quote my friend, Martha Kipcak, "This recipe has become a staple in my kitchen. Leftovers have found their way over pasta or chicken or even to simmer a tough round steak. ... Surely heaven must smell like your kitchen when this soup is cooking!"

1 whole bulb of garlic, minced
½ cup good quality olive oil
2 tablespoons dried thyme
2 teaspoons beef bouillon dissolved in 2 cups boiling water
2 28-ounce cans whole tomatoes with juice, coarsely chopped
Pepper to taste, freshly ground
Garnish: Feta cheese, crumbled

1. Sauté minced garlic in olive oil, stirring constantly, for several minutes. Be careful not to allow garlic to turn brown for this will cause a bitter flavor.
2. Add thyme, beef bouillon and tomatoes with juice.
3. Simmer soup for one hour (or longer) over low heat, allow the flavors to blend. Pepper to taste. Garnish with feta cheese.

Serves 8 to 10.

No one knows what is in the pot except the spoon that stirs the contents.

Notes

_____

_____

_____

_____

_____

_____

_____

_____

_____

_____

_____

_____

_____

Salads

Caesar Salad

I like this version of Caesar salad - fresh and light taste. Be sure the greens are crisp and cold. Enjoy!

2 heads Romaine lettuce, washed and torn into bite-size pieces
1 recipe Caesar Salad Dressing (recipe following)
Garlic Croutons (see Index)
¼ to ½ cup Parmesan cheese, grated

1. In a large salad bowl, toss all of the ingredients together.

Serves 6 to 8 as a dinner salad.
Serves 4 to 6 as a lunch entrée.

Caesar Salad Dressing

This dressing adds a wonderful zesty flavor to Caesar salads. It also makes a delicious dipping sauce for steamed artichokes - and is especially good drizzled over fresh steamed asparagus!

2 garlic cloves
1 egg*
3 tablespoons lemon juice
½ cup Romano cheese, grated
½ teaspoon pepper, freshly ground
½ teaspoon salt
½ cup olive oil

1. Combine all ingredients except oil in blender. Blend well.
2. With machine running, slowly add oil until thoroughly blended.

Makes 1 cup.

*Note: Place egg in pot of boiling water for 1 minute.

"New House" Hot Potato Salad

I made this salad to take to David and Helana's new house as a "welcome home" from their honeymoon. It's a very tasty dish - nice for potlucks or a house warming!

½ pound bacon, diced
8 cups red potatoes, cubed unpeeled
4 to 5 garlic cloves, thinly sliced
1 cup red bell pepper, thinly sliced
1 teaspoon pepper, freshly ground
⅓ cup balsamic vinegar
1 teaspoon salt

1. Brown the bacon in a skillet. Reserve 2 tablespoons bacon fat. Meanwhile, boil water to cook the potatoes.

2. Add the garlic and bell peppers to the browned bacon. Add the pepper and balsamic vinegar. Cook for a few minutes for the flavors to blend.

3. Pour the boiled potatoes into a large casserole dish. Add the bacon mixture and salt. Toss well and serve warm.

Serves 10.

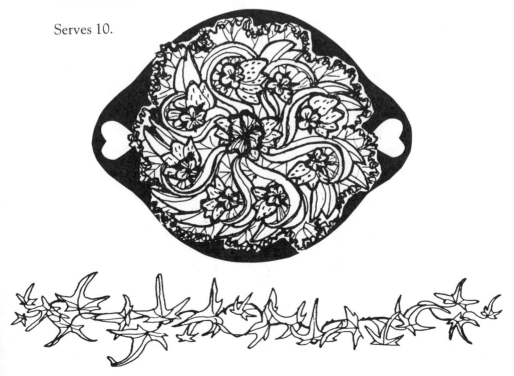

Texas Potato Salad

A hearty salad to serve with grilled meats in the summer. The flavors are more intense when it's served at room temperature. This is a wonderful addition to the Texas Salad Nicoise (recipe following).

6 red potatoes, unpeeled and sliced
1 white onion, chopped
7 green onions, chopped
1 cup dressing

1. Cook potatoes in boiling water until tender. Drain.
2. In a large bowl, combine potatoes, onions and dressing.

Serves 12.

Dressing:
⅔ cup canola oil
⅓ cup cider vinegar
4 tablespoons lemon juice
1 teaspoon ground comino
1 teaspoon pepper, freshly ground
1 teaspoon salt
¼ cup jalapeños, pickled and sliced
¼ cup fresh parsley, chopped
4 tablespoons fresh oregano leaves, chopped
4 to 5 garlic cloves, minced

Combine ingredients in blender and mix well.

Makes 1 cup.*

*Note: Reserve 2 tablespoons of dressing to use with Texas Salad Nicoise (recipe following).

Ni contigo ni sin ti.

Texas Salad Nicoise

Look for the picture of this salad with the Peach Margaritas. It is lovely arranged on a large platter for a summer buffet. Add some fresh oregano sprigs as a pretty garland. Nasturtium flowers look pretty, too.

4 lettuce leaves or a bed of mixed salad greens
⅓ cup Texas Potato Salad (recipe on opposite page)
¼ cup black beans, cooked
½ cup cooked chicken breast, sliced
1 Roma tomato
2 unpitted black olives
¼ yellow or red pepper, thinly sliced
1 hard-boiled egg, sliced
2 tablespoons Texas Potato Salad Dressing (recipe on opposite page)
Garnish: Sprigs of fresh oregano

1. Place lettuce leaves or a bed of greens on a pretty plate. On top of lettuce, layer Texas Potato Salad, then black beans. Arrange chicken slices. Top with tomato wedges, black olives, peppers, slices of hard-boiled egg. Garnish with sprigs of fresh oregano.
2. Drizzle with Texas Potato Salad Dressing.

Serves 1.

Note: The ingredients in this salad are portioned for one serving - for groups of people - proceed accordingly.

I cannot live with you nor without you.

Pasta Salad

A wonderful dish to take on picnics. While you are traveling, the pasta marinates and just gets better. For a hearty variation, toss in Italian Meatballs (see Index) and serve garnished with fresh ground Parmesan and sprigs of fresh oregano.

20 ounces of pasta (use a combination such as spiral, shells,
Orecchiette or any combination of your choosing)
½ large red onion, thinly sliced
½ red pepper, thinly sliced
½ yellow pepper, thinly sliced
3 carrots, sliced diagonally
1½ cups Balsamic Vinaigrette (see Index)
4 tablespoons fresh oregano, chopped
4 tablespoons fresh parsley, chopped
1 teaspoon pepper
1 to 2 teaspoons salt
1 cup frozen peas
2 garlic cloves, minced
4 tablespoons capers (optional)

1. Cook pasta according to package directions, drain and let cool for 10 to 15 minutes.*

2. Combine remaining ingredients.

Serves 14.

Note: It's best when served at room temperature.

*Note: Pasta is very tender and tears easily when it is first cooked. Since you will be tossing it to combine the ingredients, let it cool slightly and it will not be as delicate.

Que sea lo que Dios quiera.

Seafood Salad

A delicious luncheon dish when served over fresh salad greens. Garnish with sprigs of fresh dill and thin cucumber slices. It's also a wonderful filling for tea sandwiches - that's the way I remember them at my grandmother's garden parties in Michigan.

4 cups seafood*, cooked, coarsely chopped
4 tablespoons onion, finely chopped
2 celery stalks, finely chopped
4 green onions, finely chopped
2 tablespoon pimentos, minced
3 tablespoons fresh dill, minced
2 tablespoon capers

Dressing:

1 egg yolk
1 egg
1 garlic clove
½ teaspoon dry mustard
2 teaspoons lemon juice
½ teaspoon salt
½ teaspoon pepper
¾ cup canola oil

1. Combine the seafood, onion, celery, green onions, pimentos, dill and capers in a large bowl. Set aside.
2. In a blender, mix the egg yolk, egg, garlic, mustard, lemon juice, salt and pepper. While the blender is running, slowly add oil, allowing the dressing to thicken as the oil is added.
3. Mix the dressing into the seafood mixture.
4. Refrigerate the salad until ready to serve.

Makes 5 cups.

*Note: Use a mixture of available seafood. I like to use 2 cups shrimp, 1 cup scallops, and 1 cup crab meat.

Let God's will prevail.

Hot Chicken Salad

A really delicious "salad" served right out of a pretty casserole dish. It also makes a terrific open-faced hot sandwich - mound on a bun, with cheese and chips on top, and place in oven to bake until the cheese is melted. Set on a plate next to a cup of soup and you'll get raves of appreciation!

2 cups chicken, cooked and cubed
2 cups celery, thinly sliced
1½ cans water chestnuts, sliced
1 cup green peas, frozen
¼ cup pimento strips
⅓ cup almonds, slivered
1 cup mayonnaise
4 tablespoons lemon juice
Salt and pepper to taste
2 cups Cheddar cheese, shredded
2 cups crushed, good old-fashioned salted potato chips
Paprika

1. Preheat oven to 350 degrees.
2. Mix chicken, celery, water chestnuts, peas, pimentos and almonds with the mayonnaise and lemon juice. Salt and pepper to taste.
3. Spoon this mixture into a 2-quart casserole baking dish. Cover with the cheese and then the crushed potato chips. Sprinkle with paprika.
4. Bake for 20 minutes until heated through and the cheese melts.

Serves 6 to 8.

Der Horcher an der Wand, hort seine eigne Schand.

Gästehaus Schmidt Salad Dressing

This dressing will really dress up any salad - use it alone on salad greens, a cold vegetable platter, or as the finishing touch to a meat and vegetable platter - enjoy!

½ cup vinegar-wine, cider or malt
¾ teaspoon salt
¼ teaspoon white pepper
1½ cups olive oil
2 tablespoons hard cooked egg yolk, chopped
2 tablespoons capers, chopped
Anchovy paste the size of a pea
1 large garlic clove, finely grated
2 drops Tabasco

1. Stir together vinegar, salt, white pepper, and olive oil with a fork until thoroughly combined.

2. Add hard-cooked egg yolk, capers, anchovy paste, garlic clove and Tabasco. Mix again. (The dressing may be made in a bottle and shaken vigorously).

3. For a thicker, creamier dressing, put an ice cube into the dressing for a minute or two longer.

Makes 2 cups.

The eavesdropper usually hears something about his own shame and blame.

Balsamic Vinaigrette

This dressing is really hard to top. I make it in quantity and keep it in a pretty bottle in the fridge - so nice to have on hand!

3 garlic cloves
2 tablespoons honey
¾ cup balsamic vinegar
¼ cup water
2 teaspoons pepper
1¼ cups canola oil

1. Combine all ingredients except oil in blender. Blend well.
2. With machine running, slowly add oil until thoroughly blended.

Makes 2¼ cups.

Orange Balsamic Vinaigrette

Drizzle this dressing over fresh salad greens, garnished with orange slices, strips of beets and pistachios.

2 garlic cloves
2 teaspoons honey
1 teaspoon pommery mustard
½ cup freshly squeezed orange juice
¼ cup balsamic vinegar
½ to 1 teaspoon pepper, freshly ground
¼ cup water
1 cup oil

1. Combine all ingredients except oil in blender. Blend well.
2. With machine running, slowly add oil until thoroughly blended.

Makes 2 cups.

Side Dishes

Braised Cabbage

I made this dish last summer when I had a gorgeous assortment of fresh veg-etables from Marianne and Steve's organic farm in Dripping Springs. I wanted to enjoy some of everything at once ... and this is the wonderful recipe that resulted that day.

I repeat this recipe often, and sometimes it changes a little because of the avail-ability or discovery of new vegetables.

2 tablespoons olive oil
4 garlic cloves, thinly sliced
1 leek, coarsely chopped
½ head cabbage, thinly sliced
1 medium sweet potato, peeled and cubed
1 small turnip, sliced
1 red pepper, sliced
1 medium acorn squash, unpeeled, ½" slices
3 tablespoons balsamic vinegar
Pepper to taste, freshly ground
Salt to taste

1. In a large pot, place olive oil and garlic, cook slowly until tender. Add leeks and cook for about 2 minutes.

2. Layer the remaining ingredients in pot, over leeks. Begin with cabbage, sweet potatoes, turnips, red pepper, then rings of acorn squash.

3. Add balsamic vinegar and freshly ground pepper.

4. Cover tightly and cook over medium heat for 25 to 30 minutes until vegetables are tender. Stir gently just before serving. Taste for salt and pepper.

Serves 8.

*Note: There is a really good sausage being made which is becoming available in some of the specialty food stores - chicken and apple sausage. If you are fortunate enough to find it, add it to this recipe during cooking - or any other good quality sausage is good, too!

Red Cabbage

An excellent dish to serve with roasted pork tenderloin or Sauerbraten and it adds such a pretty rich color on the plate!

2 to 3 slices bacon, diced
½ medium onion, sliced
1 Granny Smith apple, sliced and peeled
1 medium head red cabbage (6 cups), sliced
¼ cup brown sugar
1 teaspoon salt
½ cup red wine vinegar

1. Sauté bacon. Add onion, apple and sauté for 1 minute.
2. Add remaining ingredients.
3. Cook, covered, for 45 minutes to 1 hour.

Serves 6.

Jo's Garlic Spaghetti

My aunt shared this recipe with me when I was first married. It's a very easy dish to prepare. My children were always delighted to see it appear on our supper table when they were young.

1 10-ounce package thin spaghetti
3 tablespoons butter
3 tablespoons olive oil
6 garlic cloves, minced
Salt and pepper to taste
Garnish: Parmesan, freshly grated

1. Cook spaghetti according to package instructions.
2. Meanwhile, melt butter with olive oil in large skillet, add garlic and cook over medium heat until garlic is soft and light brown.
3. Drain spaghetti and immediately add to skillet with garlic mixture. Taste for salt and pepper. Toss well and serve. Garnish with fresh grated Parmesan.

Serves 6.

Garlic Roasted Potatoes

When serving these for a buffet, place on a pretty platter with a garland of fresh rosemary. This is a delicious way to prepare potatoes - and very exciting to catch the aroma when the parchment is opened! - and what's more, there's no pot to clean!

1½ pounds unpeeled red potatoes, cut into 1½" cubes
1 teaspoon pepper, freshly ground
1 teaspoon salt
2 teaspoons balsamic vinegar
4 to 5 rosemary sprigs
4 garlic cloves, thinly sliced
2 to 3 tablespoons olive oil

1. Preheat oven to 400 degrees.
2. Mix together all ingredients and toss until potatoes are coated.
3. Wrap ingredients in parchment.
4. Bake for 1 hour.

Variation:
These can be removed from the parchment into an oven proof casserole and placed under the broiler for several minutes until they become crusty.

Serves 6 to 8.

Wie die Alten sungen so zwitschern die Jungen.

Potato Cakes

These are a good side dish when you entertain - they can be formed early in the day and kept in the refrigerator. Cook as much as 2 hours before serving. Place on a baking sheet and hold until serving time. Reheat until crisp in 350 degree oven for 10 to 15 minutes just before serving time. Garnish on a platter with fresh parsley.

2 large russet potatoes, peeled, cooked, grated
2 eggs, beaten
6 to 8 green onions, chopped
3 garlic cloves, minced
2 teaspoons ground comino
1 teaspoon salt
1 teaspoon pepper
Paprika
3 tablespoons olive oil
2 tablespoons butter
Garnish: Fresh parsley

1. Boil potatoes unpeeled in a large pot of water until just done. Do not overcook. Drain and let cool.
2. Mix eggs, and green onions. Add garlic, comino, salt and pepper.
3. Peel and grate potatoes and gently stir into egg mixture.
4. Form into 3" patties. Sprinkle generously with paprika.*
5. Heat oil and butter in skillet. Place potato cakes in hot oil mixture, sauté until golden and serve.

Makes about 12 cakes. Serves 6.

*Note: Paprika adds nice flavor and also helps speed up the browning process when sautéing potato cakes, chicken breasts or fish filets!

As the old ones sing— so whistle the younger ones.

Garlic Mashed Potatoes

I serve these potatoes often to company and my family. They can be prepared several hours ahead. Cover tightly with a cover or aluminum foil. Heat in a moderate oven for about 20 to 30 minutes. Remove cover just before serving.

4 pounds red potatoes, cut into 1 inch pieces, unpeeled
4 to 6 large garlic cloves, whole
1 cup milk
½ cup butter
Salt and pepper to taste
4 large garlic cloves, thinly sliced
1 tablespoon olive oil

1. Place potatoes and garlic cloves in a large pot. Cover with water and bring to a boil. Cook until potatoes are tender, about 12 to 15 minutes.

2. Drain potatoes and garlic. Mash until the large lumps are gone. (This is where personal preference comes in - I really prefer some lumps in my mashed potatoes!) Add milk and butter and beat well to combine. Add salt and pepper to taste. Place in a baking dish.

3. In a small skillet, sauté the sliced garlic with the olive oil until light golden brown. Sprinkle garlic and oil over the mashed potatoes. Serve...and relish the raves you'll receive!!!

Serves 8 to 10.

**Des menschen Gluck auf Erden ist lieben
und geliebt zu werden.**

Sweet Potato Souffle with Sherry and Walnuts

We serve these sweet potatoes at Thanksgiving and Christmas. They are lighter than the candied yams that we enjoyed when I was growing up at home. It's a dish I find myself doing often.

4 cups sweet potatoes, cooked and mashed
⅓ cup dry sherry
¼ to ½ teaspoon salt
⅓ cup brown sugar
2 eggs, beaten
½ cup walnuts, toasted and chopped
2 tablespoons butter
½ teaspoon nutmeg
1 tablespoon brown sugar

1. Preheat oven to 325 degrees.

2. Using an electric mixer, blend sweet potatoes, sherry, salt, brown sugar and eggs, until light and fluffy.

3. Pour into a 8" x 12" greased casserole dish and top with walnuts. Dot with butter and sprinkle with nutmeg and brown sugar. Bake uncovered for 25 to 30 minutes.

Serves 8 to 10.

It is the good fortune of man on earth to love and be loved in return.

Rice Pilaf

A great side dish to serve with chicken or fish. The lentils cook along with the rice and provide flavor, nutrition and interest.

1 cup rice*
1 tablespoon olive oil
1 tablespoon butter
1 small onion, chopped
1 large garlic clove, sliced thin
3 cups chicken broth
½ cup dried lentils, sorted and rinsed
½ to 1 teaspoon curry powder
1 teaspoon salt

1. In a sauce pan, brown rice in olive oil and butter together with onion and garlic. Cook and stir until onions are soft and rice is light golden brown.
2. Add remaining ingredients. Cover and simmer for 25 minutes.

Serves 4.

*Note: Long grain rice mixed with wild rice is great!

Caraway Noodles

Try these noodles when you serve Sauerbraten (see Index) or a hearty beef stew. It's a tasty complement and so simple!

1 teaspoon salt
1 8-ounce package medium noodles
¼ cup butter, melted
1 tablespoon caraway seeds

1. Prepare noodles according to package directions.
2. Add butter and caraway seeds, toss lightly to combine.

Serves 6.

Baked Macaroni with Italian Cheeses

This is Tina's fancy version of macaroni and cheese. It's good enough to stand alone as an entrée - just add a great salad and crusty bread!

1 cup fresh bread crumbs
⅓ cup Parmesan cheese
2 tablespoons parsley, minced
1 teaspoon paprika
6 tablespoons butter, melted
12 ounces elbow macaroni
1 small onion, minced
2 tablespoons flour
2 cups milk
2 cups Provolone cheese, shredded
½ cup Gorgonzola cheese, crumbled
1 cup fontina cheese, grated
½ teaspoon nutmeg
Pepper, freshly ground
1 teaspoon paprika

1. In a small bowl, mix together the bread crumbs, Parmesan, parsley, paprika and 2 tablespoons butter. Set aside to use for topping later.

2. Preheat oven to 375 degrees.

3. Cook macaroni according to package directions. Rinse under cool water and set aside.

4. In a medium saucepan, sauté the onion in 4 tablespoons butter until transparent. Add the flour and cook, while stirring, for one minute. Then add milk and simmer for 5 minutes, stirring occasionally.

5. Add cooked macaroni with the cheeses, and nutmeg. Continue to simmer for 5 to 10 minutes until cheese has melted.

6. Grease a 9" x 13" casserole dish. Pour macaroni and cheese into the dish. Sprinkle bread crumb mixture evenly over top. Grind pepper on top. Sprinkle with paprika for color. Bake for 25 to 30 minutes until light brown and bubbly. Serve hot.

Serves 8 to 10.

Pinto Beans

This recipe seems almost too obvious to put into a cookbook. But when Hector and I were first married, I had not the slightest idea how to cook beans. This is the way Hector showed me to cook pinto beans. His mother used to add bacon or salt pork, but they are just as good without it.

3 cups dried pinto beans, or red beans
8 cups water
4 large garlic cloves, minced
2 teaspoons salt

1. Place beans, water and garlic in a stock pot. Bring to a boil. Turn heat to low and let the beans cook for 2 to 3 hours. Add water as needed, 2 cups at a time.
2. Just before done, add salt. Continue cooking until beans are soft. The cooking time can vary depending on how fresh your beans are.

Makes 10 cups.

Borraccho Beans

Borraccho is Spanish for "drunken" beans - it's the beer! These are great to serve by the bowlful with Corn Muffins (see Index). They also work well in the Bean Cake recipe (recipe following), if you have some left!

3 cups pinto beans
10 cups water
2 to 3 slices bacon, diced
2 tablespoons olive oil
1 medium onion, chopped
6 garlic cloves, minced
1 14½-ounce can tomatoes, chopped
1 can beer
3 to 4 tablespoons pickled jalapeños, chopped
1 teaspoon salt
2 teaspoons ground comino

Panza llena, corazón contento.

1. Cook beans, water and bacon for 1 hour.

2. Sauté in olive oil, onion and garlic. Add to beans.

3. Add remaining ingredients and continue cooking until beans are very tender, about 2 more hours.

Makes 10 to 12 cups.

Bean Cakes

These are fantastic as a first course or as a side dish - also just as a fun snack. Top them with Tomatillo Salsa (see Index) when you serve them - muy delicioso!

4 cups Pinto Beans or Borraccho Beans (opposite page)
2 eggs
½ cup bean juice
4 to 6 tablespoons oil
Garnish: Sour cream, green onions, finely chopped

1. Place beans in food processor until coarsely chopped.

2. Add eggs, beans and juice until combined.

3. Heat 2 tablespoons oil in skillet. Drop beans by spoonfuls - about ⅓ cup - fry until golden, turning once. Add remaining oil as needed.

4. Remove from skillet. Place on baking sheet in a 250 degree oven until all are completed and ready to serve. Garnish with a dollop of sour cream and sprinkle with finely chopped green onion.

Note: For special individual appetizers when serving a Southwestern menu - place Bean Cake on a pool of Chili Poblano Soup (see Index). Top with a dollop of Creme Fraîche (see Index) and a sprig of cilantro.

Makes about 14 cakes.

Full stomach, happy heart.

Scalloped Oyster Dressing

I don't think we've ever spent a Christmas without serving Oyster Dressing. My grandmother prepared it every year - and when she couldn't manage any longer, my mother took over the tradition. Now I make it for my family. There was never a recipe until now - I'm so glad I paid attention and learned how it's done.

3 cups saltines, crushed (not fine)
2 10-ounce jars fresh oysters, drained, reserve 4 tablespoons of liquid
2 tablespoons butter
Pepper, freshly ground
1 cup milk
2 eggs
Dash of Tabasco
1 cup soft bread crumbs, coarse
2 tablespoons butter, softened
1 teaspoon paprika

1. Preheat oven to 400 degrees.
2. In a 10" casserole, which has been sprayed with non stick spray, layer crackers, then oysters mixed with reserved liquid. Dot with 2 tablespoons butter. Add freshly ground pepper.
3. Mix together milk, eggs and Tabasco. Pour over oyster-cracker mixture.
4. In bowl of food processor, process bread crumbs, butter and paprika. Pulse several times to distribute paprika and butter through crumbs. Spread over oyster-cracker-milk combination. Add a few grindings of fresh pepper.
5. Bake for 20 to 25 minutes.

Serves 4 to 6.

Note: When I was testing this recipe, my friend, Joanie, made a wonderful serving suggestion: place each serving on a bed of wilted spinach greens, and garnish with a lemon twist. It's not just for Christmas anymore at the Pedregons!

Cynthia's Corn Bread Dressing

I learned to make this dressing by watching, and later helping my mother every holiday when I was growing up. Family traditions have always been important to me. I feel it's lots of little things that we do together that make our families unique and give us a strong sense of belonging to one another, even when we're away from "home".

When Hector and I were living in Puerto Rico - my first Thanksgiving away from my family - we went to the beach while the turkey was roasting in the oven. The turkey was stuffed, of course, with this same "Collins" stuffing!

¼ pound butter
3 cups celery, coarsely chopped
1 medium onion, coarsely chopped
1 cup mushrooms, sliced
2 boiled eggs, sliced
1 8-ounce can water chestnuts, sliced
1 recipe Ottis' Corn Bread (see Index), cubed
½ cup fresh parsley, coarsely chopped
Salt and pepper to taste
2 eggs
½ cup pecans, cashews or peanuts (optional)
1 apple, unpeeled, chopped
3 cups chicken broth
2 to 3 tablespoons butter
Paprika

1. Melt ¼ pound butter in large skillet. Add celery, onion, mushrooms and cook over medium heat until tender.

2. Add remaining ingredients and mix well.

3. Pour into a 9" x 13" baking pan and dot with 2 to 3 tablespoons butter. Sprinkle generously with paprika.

4. Bake for 45 minutes.

Serves 12 to 14.

Note: When I stuff a 16 to 18 pound turkey (packing it loosely), I sometimes have extra dressing. I bake the remaining dressing in a small casserole and combine the two quantities when I serve.

Notes

Quiches

Basic Quiche Crust

We use this basic crust recipe for all of our quiches in the Tea Room. We make several ahead of time and store them in the freezer until ready to use - it's a good time saver!

1½ cups unsifted unbleached flour
½ teaspoon salt
2 tablespoons Crisco shortening
6 tablespoons CHILLED butter (not margarine)
5 tablespoons ICED water

1. Mix flour and salt in bowl. Cut in Crisco and butter with a pastry blender until crumbly.

2. Add ICED water, a little at a time, mixing with a fork until well blended. Place dough into plastic bag and gently press dough together into a flat disk. Seal bag. Refrigerate dough for 30 to 60 minutes. This allows the gluten to develop in the dough.

3. On floured board, carefully roll dough to fit quiche pan 10" in diameter by 2" deep. Carefully lift into pan, trimming dough, and rolling edge under to form a rim. Flute the edge.

4. Put a layer of foil over dough and fill to the top with either pie weights or dry pinto beans. This prevents crust from puffing up and shrinking.

5. Bake crust for 15 minutes in a preheated 400 degree oven.

6. Remove beans and foil, prick crust bottom with fork several times, and bake 10 more minutes at 400 degrees. The quiche crust is now ready for filling. Reduce temperature of oven to 350 degrees.

Makes 1 quiche crust, 10" diameter x 2" deep.

Schuster bleib bei deinem Leisten.

Deviled Eggs, Steamed Asparagus and Artichokes with Caesar Salad
Dressing for Dipping

Brie in Brioche

the Peach Tree Tea Room

Clarified Butter

This recipe is a repeat from our first cookbook. I wanted to include it here because of the technique used. Many of our quiche recipes call for clarified butter - it's very nice to have on hand (I keep mine in the freezer).

The advantage of using clarified butter is that it will not burn when sautéing at high temperatures. It would be time-saving to clarify several pounds of butter at a time.

1. Place 1 pound butter (not margarine) in a large Pyrex measuring cup. Microwave the butter for 2 minutes on high until melted. This can also be done on the stove in a saucepan, taking care that the butter does not burn.

2. Place the measuring cup in the freezer and freeze until the butter is solid. Using the point of a sharp knife, lift the frozen butter from the measuring cup. Gently rinse the butter solid under cold running water to remove all the foamy milk solids.

3. Blot the butter with paper towels. Cut into small chunks, if desired, and store in a plastic bag in the freezer. You may want to cut the block into 1 tablespoon pieces.

Shoemaker stay with your trade.

Leek and Mushroom Quiche

The leeks and mushrooms are an interesting flavor combination. A nice varia-tion would be to add 1½ cups of steamed asparagus as the top layer.

1 recipe Basic Quiche Crust, 10" x 2", partially baked
according to directions
2 cups leek, chopped
2 cups mushrooms, sliced
2 garlic cloves, minced
1 tablespoon Clarified Butter (see previous page), margarine or
cooking oil
10 eggs
1 teaspoon white pepper
1 teaspoon salt
½ cup ricotta cheese
8 ounces cream cheese
2½ cups evaporated milk
⅔ cup Swiss cheese, shredded

1. Preheat oven to 350 degrees.
2. Sauté leeks, mushrooms and garlic in butter, margarine or cooking oil.
3. Beat eggs in blender with white pepper, salt, ricotta cheese and cream cheese.
4. Add milk to egg mixture.
5. In prepared crust, place half of Swiss cheese on bottom. Layer with the leek and mushroom mixture and finish with the remaining Swiss cheese.
6. Pour egg mixture over layered ingredients.
7. Bake for 1 hour and 45 minutes, or until knife inserted in center comes out clean. Allow quiche to cool for 15 minutes for easier slicing.

Serves 9 to 10.

Para entrar al cielo, tienes que ser como un niño.

Chicken Artichoke Quiche

A nice quiche for a luncheon - the flavors are delicate and light. Serve with a tossed green salad, topped with an Orange Balsamic Vinaigrette (see Index), and Blueberry-Pecan Corn Muffins (see Index).

1 recipe Basic Quiche Crust, 10" x 2", partially baked
according to directions
10 eggs
1 teaspoon garlic, minced
1 teaspoon salt
1 teaspoon white pepper
2 to 2½ cups evaporated milk
2 cups Swiss cheese, shredded
1 cup chicken, cooked and cubed, soaked in 3 tablespoons dry
sherry several hours or overnight.
1 cup artichoke hearts, quartered
1 cup green onions, chopped

1. Preheat oven to 350 degrees.
2. Beat eggs in blender with garlic, salt, and white pepper.
3. Add milk to egg mixture.
4. In prepared crust, place half of cheese on the bottom. Layer with the chicken, artichokes and onions. Sprinkle with remaining cheese.
5. Pour egg and milk mixture over the layered ingredients.
6. Bake for 1 hour and 45 minutes or until knife inserted in center comes out clean. Allow quiche to cool 15 minutes for easier slicing.

Serves 9 to 10.

To enter heaven, you must be like a child.

Southwest Quiche

Santa Fe Corn Soup is one of our most popular soups from the first Peach Tree Cookbook - so we decided to use the same combination of ingredients for this quiche. It's delicious and another one that men really enjoy!

1 recipe Basic Quiche Crust, 10" x 2", partially baked according to directions
½ cup purple onion, sliced
½ teaspoon garlic, minced
1 tablespoon Clarified Butter (see Index), margarine or cooking oil
10 eggs
1 teaspoon salt
1 teaspoon white pepper
1 teaspoon ground comino
1 teaspoon garlic, minced
1 teaspoon jalapeños
2 to 2½ cups evaporated milk
2 cups Monterey Jack cheese, shredded
1 cup chicken, cooked and cubed
1 cup green chilies, sliced in strips
1 cup corn
1 whole pimento, sliced in strips

1. Preheat oven to 350 degrees.
2. Sauté onion and garlic in butter, margarine or cooking oil.
3. Beat eggs in blender with salt, white pepper, comino, garlic, and jalapeños.
4. Add milk to egg mixture.
5. In prepared crust, place half of cheese on bottom. Layer with chicken, green chilies, corn, sautéed onion mixture, and pimentos. Sprinkle with remaining cheese.
6. Pour egg mixture over layered ingredients.
7. Bake for 1 hour and 45 minutes, or until knife inserted in center comes out clean. Allow quiche to cool for 15 minutes for easier slicing.

Serves 9 to 10.

Tomatillo Quiche

The tomatillos offer a nice flavor combined with the cilantro and green chilies. I think this makes an outstanding quiche.

1 recipe Basic Quiche Crust, 10" x 2", partially baked according to directions
1 cup red onions, sliced
2 garlic cloves, minced
2 tablespoons Clarified Butter (see Index), margarine or cooking oil
10 eggs
1 teaspoon white pepper
1 teaspoon salt
1 teaspoon ground comino
1 teaspoon jalapeños, sliced
2 cups milk
1 tablespoon fresh cilantro
2 cups Monterey Jack cheese, shredded
1 cup green chilies, sliced
1 cup cooked tomatillos, coarsely chopped and drained
1½ cups chicken, cooked and cubed
Garnish: Sour cream, black olives, and cilantro sprigs.

1. Preheat oven to 350 degrees.
2. Sauté onions and garlic in butter, margarine or cooking oil.
3. Beat eggs in blender with white pepper, salt, comino, and jalapeños.
4. Add milk and cilantro to egg mixture.
5. In prepared crust place half of the cheese on the bottom. Layer with onion-garlic mixture, chilies, tomatillos, and chicken, and finish with the remaining cheese.
6. Pour egg and milk mixture over the layered ingredients.
7. Bake for 1 hour and 45 minutes or until knife inserted in the center comes out clean. Allow quiche to cool 15 minutes for easier slicing. Garnish with a dollop of sour cream, a black olive, and a sprig of cilantro.

Serves 9 to 10.

Italian Sausage Quiche

A fresh baked quiche is a great idea for picnics - and this one with Italian sausage would be especially appetizing. Serve with a Caesar salad and a loaf of French or Tuscan bread. Be sure to pack a bottle of good red wine and your outdoor feast is complete!

1 recipe Basic Quiche Crust, 10" x 2", partially baked
according to directions
8 ounces Italian sausage
1 10-ounce package frozen, chopped spinach, thawed
10 eggs
½ cup ricotta cheese
1 teaspoon salt
1 teaspoon white pepper
2 to 2½ cups evaporated milk
2 cups Swiss cheese, shredded
1 cup green onions, chopped
Fresh tomato slices
Romano cheese, grated

1. Preheat oven to 350 degrees.
2. Sauté sausage. Drain off the extra grease by placing the cooked sausage on a paper towel. Slice sausage and drain again.
3. Remove all moisture from spinach. Wrap in clean cotton towel and squeeze dry.
4. Beat eggs in blender with ricotta, salt and pepper.
5. Add milk to egg mixture.
6. In prepared crust, place half of Swiss cheese on bottom. Layer green onions, spinach and sausage over the Swiss cheese. Sprinkle with remaining Swiss cheese.
7. Pour egg mixture over the layered ingredients.
8. Top with tomato slices and sprinkle with Romano Cheese.
9. Bake for 1 hour and 30 minutes, or until knife inserted comes out clean. Allow quiche to cool 15 minutes for easier slicing.

Serves 9 to 10.

Fredericksburg Quiche

Octoberfest in Fredericksburg was the inspiration for this quiche. We use Opa's Sausage which is made locally, and we are very fortunate to have it. If it is not available in your area, feel free to use a good quality German smoked sausage. This is a hearty quiche and very popular with our "real men" at The Peach Tree!

1 recipe Basic Quiche Crust, 10" x 2", partially baked according to directions
¾ cup red onion, sliced
2 garlic cloves, minced
¾ cup green bell pepper, chopped
1 tablespoon Clarified Butter (see Index), margarine or cooking oil
1 cup Opa's Sausage, sliced
¾ cup zucchini, sliced
10 eggs
1 teaspoon salt
1 teaspoon white pepper
½ cup cream cheese
2 to 2½ cups evaporated milk
2 cups Swiss cheese, shredded

1. Preheat oven to 350 degrees.
2. Sauté onion, garlic and bell pepper in butter, margarine or cooking oil. When onions are tender, add sausage slices and continue to cook until the sausage begins to brown. Add zucchini and continue cooking until just tender.
3. Beat eggs in blender with salt, white pepper, and cream cheese.
4. Add milk to egg mixture.
5. In prepared crust, place half of Swiss cheese on bottom layer with the sautéed vegetables and sausage and finish with the remaining cheese.
6. Pour egg mixture over layered ingredients.
7. Bake for 1 hour and 30 minutes, or until knife inserted in center comes out clean. Allow quiche to cool for 15 minutes for easier slicing.

Serves 9 to 10.

Jalapeño-Potato Quiche

I love the combination of potatoes, jalapeños, garlic and bacon. It is terrific served with fresh fruit for breakfast or brunch.

1 recipe Basic Quiche Crust, 10" x 2" partially baked
according to directions
1 cup onion, sliced
½ pound bacon, diced
10 eggs
1 tablespoon garlic
1 teaspoon ground comino
1 teaspoon pepper, freshly ground
1 teaspoon salt
2½ cups evaporated milk
2 cups Cheddar cheese, shredded
1½ cups cooked potatoes, cubed
½ cup pimentos, chopped
¼ to ½ cup jalapeños with juice, sliced
Garnish: Sour cream and green onions, finely chopped.

1. Preheat oven to 350 degrees.
2. Sauté onions with bacon. Drain well.
3. Beat eggs in blender with garlic, comino, pepper, and salt.
4. Add milk to egg mixture.
5. In prepared crust, layer half of cheese on the bottom. Then layer the potatoes, bacon and onions, pimentos and jalapeños with juice. Sprinkle with the remaining cheese.
6. Pour the egg mixture over the layered ingredients.
7. Bake for 1 hour and 45 minutes, or until knife inserted in the center comes out clean. Allow quiche to cool 15 minutes for easier slicing. Garnish with a dollop of sour cream and a sprinkle of chopped green onions.

Serves 9 to 10.

Entrees

Shrimp Strudel

A twist on the Austrian Chicken Strudel from our first cookbook - you'll enjoy this variation. I also like to use Lappi cheese with this version in place of the Swiss cheese - both are delicious!

4 green onions, chopped
⅓ pound fresh mushrooms, sliced
2 tablespoons butter
4 cups cooked shrimp, coarsely chopped
½ teaspoon salt
¼ teaspoon pepper, freshly ground
2 tablespoons fresh parsley, chopped
½ teaspoon tarragon
2 eggs
1½ cups Swiss cheese, shredded
16 sheets filo pastry
½ cup butter, melted
Garnish: Sour cream

1. Preheat oven to 400 degrees.
2. Sauté onions and mushrooms in butter until tender.
3. In a bowl, combine the onion-mushroom mixture, shrimp, salt, pepper, parsley, and tarragon. Stir in eggs and cheese.
4. Lay out 1 sheet of filo pastry and brush with melted butter. Place another sheet of filo pastry on top of the first and brush with butter.
5. Spoon ⅔ cup of shrimp filling along one end of the rectangle, leaving a margin of 2" in from the end as well as both sides. Fold in both ends and loosely roll up the strudel. Brush with butter and place on a greased baking sheet. Repeat this process until all filling is used.
6. Bake for 35 minutes, or until crust is golden brown. Garnish with a dollop of sour cream.

Serves 8.

Strudel de Pescadillo

Pescadillo is Spanish for "little fish" - all the "little fish" I truly enjoy - shrimp, scallops, crabs. Layered with filo pastry leaves, it is an easy-to-make and elegant entrée.

2 garlic cloves, minced
6 green onions, chopped
2 tablespoons butter
1½ pounds shrimp, cooked and coarsely chopped
8 ounces sea scallops, sliced in half, cooked
4 ounces crabmeat, cooked
1 cup green chilies, chopped
½ cup black olives, sliced
½ teaspoon salt
½ teaspoon pepper, freshly ground
1 to 2 teaspoons ground comino
3 eggs
1½ cups Monterey Jack cheese, shredded
½ cup melted butter
20 sheets filo pastry
Garnish: Sour cream

1. Preheat oven to 400 degrees.
2. Sauté the garlic and onions in 2 tablespoons butter until tender.
3. In a bowl, combine the garlic and onions with the shrimp, scallops, crabmeat, chilies, olives, salt, pepper and comino. Stir in the eggs and cheese.
4. In a 10" x 13" baking pan, brush butter on the bottom and sides of the dish. Count out 20 sheets of pastry and cut in half width-wise.
5. Begin by laying one piece of filo pastry flat in the dish. Brush melted butter onto the dough. Repeat this process until 10 layers have been buttered. Spoon the filling over the layers and spread evenly. Lay a sheet of filo pastry over the filling and brush with melted butter. Repeat this process until 10 more layers have been buttered, including the top layer.
6. Cut into squares and bake for 35 minutes, or until the crust is golden brown. Garnish with sour cream.

Serves 8 to 10.

Seafood Lasagna

Delicate and light flavors - the Lappi cheese is a perfect cheese for seafood. The colors in this lasagna make a pretty pastel presentation. Garnish each portion with an oregano sprig and a pink begonia or geranium flower.

1 pound lasagna noodles, cooked
4 cups leeks
2 cups mushrooms, sliced
4 garlic cloves, thinly sliced
2 tablespoons olive oil
1 red pepper, sliced
1 pound shrimp, cooked
12 ounces scallops, cooked
2 eggs, beaten
6 ounces Lappi cheese, grated
1 recipe Bechamel Sauce (see Index)
3 cups Tina's Italian Pizza Sauce (see Index)
6 ounces mozzarella cheese, sliced

1. Preheat oven to 350 degrees.
2. Cook noodles according to package directions.
3. Sauté leeks, mushrooms and garlic in olive oil until tender.
4. Add pepper and cook for 1 minute until crisp tender. Stir in shrimp and scallops. Set aside for assembly.
5. Stir eggs and cheese into Bechamel Sauce. Set aside for assembly.

Assembly:
1. Coat 9" x 13" casserole dish with nonstick spray.
2. Pour in ¼ cup pizza sauce.
3. Add one layer lasagna noodles.
4. Pour on 1¼ cup pizza sauce.
5. Layer shrimp-scallop-vegetable mixture.
6. Next add the Bechamel Sauce-cheese-eggs mixture.
7. Add another layer of lasagna noodles
8. Pour on remaining pizza sauce.
9. Top with mozzarella slices.

Bake for 1 hour.

Serves 10.

Texas Strudel

Plan to do this for a summer party. It can be done a day before - and baked when ready for your guests. A nice extra is to pour Tomatillo Salsa (see Index) over top of each serving as a flavorful garnish.

6 green onions, finely chopped
2 tablespoons butter
4 cups chicken breasts, cooked, cubed
½ teaspoon salt
¼ teaspoon pepper
2 tablespoons fresh parsley, chopped
2 teaspoons ground comino
1 teaspoon garlic, minced
2 eggs
1½ cups Monterey Jack cheese, shredded
2 cups green chilies
½ cup black olives, halved
½ cup golden raisins
½ cup almonds, chopped
20 sheets filo pastry
½ cup butter, melted
Garnish: Sour cream and black olives; or fresh sprig of
oregano or cilantro.

1. Preheat oven to 400 degrees.
2. Sauté onions in butter until tender.
3. In a bowl, combine the sautéed onion, chicken, salt, pepper, parsley, comino and garlic. Stir in the eggs, cheese, chilies, olives, raisins and almonds.
4. In a 9" x 13" baking dish, brush butter on the sides and the bottom. Cut filo pastry sheets in half width-wise.
5. Begin by laying one piece of filo pastry flat in the dish. Brush melted butter onto the dough. Repeat this process until 10 layers have been buttered. Spoon the filling over the layers and spread evenly. Lay a sheet of filo pastry over the filling and brush with melted butter. Repeat this process until 10 more layers have been buttered, including the top layer. Cut into desired serving sizes before baking.
6. Bake for 35 minutes, or until the crust is golden brown. Garnish with a dollop of sour cream and a black olive, or with a fresh sprig of oregano or cilantro.

Serves 8 to 10.

Baked Chicken - Aunt Jo's Way

My Aunt Jo's chicken was always really special and set apart from any other I've tasted. Her's is so simple - it's hard to believe the difference is in such a simple addition as paprika! When I visited her in Michigan she would always bake two chickens, one for dinner and one for chicken salad later!

This recipe with the hominy is an outstanding dish. If, however, you want a simple baked chicken, omit the hominy step. Another way I like to prepare this chicken is to omit the hominy and place a whole lemon (pierce with knife about 6 times to release lemon flavor) into the cavity of the chicken along with a handful of fresh herbs, such as Italian parsley and oregano.

1 3½ to 4-pound chicken fryer
½ teaspoon salt
1 teaspoon pepper
Paprika
1 30-ounce can golden hominy

1. Preheat oven to 375 degrees.
2. Remove giblets from chicken and wash with cool running water - remove any fatty deposits.
3. Place chicken in a 9" x 13" casserole pan, breast side down. Sprinkle chicken with ½ teaspoon pepper and sprinkle liberally with paprika.
4. Place in oven and bake, uncovered for 30 minutes.
5. Remove from oven, and turn chicken breast side up. Sprinkle with remaining ½ teaspoon pepper, salt, and lots of paprika. Add hominy and return to oven. Bake for 45 minutes until chicken is golden.
6. Remove from oven, let rest 15 minutes before carving chicken.

Serves 4 to 6.

Que no te hagan de chivo los tamales.

Chicken Spaghetti

The secret to this recipe is keeping the ingredients crisp-tender to prevent their getting mushy in the baking. It's a good dish to take to someone just home from the hospital.

1 12-ounce box spaghetti
2 slices bacon, diced
1 bell pepper, chopped
1 cup celery, chopped
1 large onion, chopped
2 cups mushrooms, sliced
1 2-ounce jar chopped pimentos
2½ to 3 cups cooked chicken
1 teaspoon pepper
Salt to taste
1 13-ounce can evaporated milk
1 10 ¾-ounce can Cream of Chicken and Mushroom Soup
1 10 ¾-ounce can Cream of Chicken Soup
8 ounces Cheddar cheese, shredded

1. Preheat oven to 350 degrees.
2. Cook the spaghetti according to package directions. Drain and place in a greased 9" x 13" baking dish and set aside.
3. In a skillet, sauté the bacon until browned and sauté the bell pepper, celery, onion, mushrooms and pimentos until crisp tender. Stir in chicken pieces until blended. Add pepper. Taste for salt. Pour chicken-vegetable mixture over spaghetti.
4. In a bowl, mix the milk and soups to make a sauce and pour over spaghetti. Top with cheese and bake for 20 to 30 minutes until heated thoroughly and cheese is melted. Can be frozen.

Serves 8 to 10.

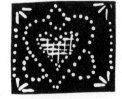

Do not let them sell you tamales made of goat meat.

Chile con Queso

*When Hector and I were first married and visited his family in El Paso, I was so surprised to see what they called Chile con Queso. Until then, I thought Chili con Queso was made with **red** chili - they prepared it with **green** chili. This turned out to be a terrific discovery. If you've never tried this version, you're in for a real treat!*

It makes a great meal when you serve it with beans and tortillas. Think of it as a green chile stew. It's also great as an appetizer served with tortilla chips for dipping or as a topping on baked potatoes!

1 small onion
2 garlic cloves, minced
2 tablespoons olive oil
1 14½-ounce can tomatoes, diced and drained
1½ cups green chilies, peeled
½ teaspoon salt
½ teaspoon pepper
2 cups Queso Asadero*
2 cups milk

1. Sauté onion and garlic in the olive oil until soft. Add the tomatoes, green chilies, salt and pepper. Simmer together for 15 minutes.
2. Add cheese, stirring until it begins to melt. Add milk.

*Note: See if you can find this wonderful Mexican white cheese - if not, use Monterey Jack cheese.

Note: Also, fresh roasted green chilies are the absolute best, but the canned green ones work really well.

Serves 6 as entrée.
Serves 20 as appetizer.

Si no te quieres quemar, salte de la cocina.

Chicken Roasted in Parchment

This is a delicious way to prepare chicken. It can be done a day ahead and kept in the fridge until ready to bake. All the juices and flavors are sealed inside the parchment, resulting in a very moist, flavorful and LOW FAT meal perfect for company or just a busy day! Place the individual packets on each plate and let each person open his own at serving time.

4 boneless chicken breasts
2 medium zucchini, thinly sliced, lengthwise
1 red pepper, thinly sliced
4 tablespoons goat cheese, optional
4 tablespoons Sun-dried Tomato Pesto (see Index) or pesto of your choice
4 sheets baking parchment

1. Preheat oven to 450 degrees.
2. Divide the ingredients into four individual portions.
3. Place one chicken breast on a parchment sheet and layer the zucchini, peppers and goat cheese; then top with pesto. Fold the parchment and twist the ends to seal. Repeat process for the other three servings.
4. Place individual packets on baking sheet and bake for 20 minutes.
5. Remove from oven and allow packets to rest 5 to 10 minutes before serving.

Makes 4 individual servings.

If you do not want to get burned, get out of the kitchen.

Chicken and Dumplings

Pure comfort food at it's old fashioned best!!

1 3 to 4-pound chicken
4 quarts water
2 teaspoons salt
2 teaspoons pepper
1 pound bag carrots, peeled, sliced into 2" lengths
1 bunch celery, (leaves included) sliced into 2" lengths
1 medium onion, coarsely chopped
½ cup fresh parsley, chopped
1 recipe Herb Dumplings (recipe following)

1. Combine chicken, water, salt and pepper. Cook for 1 hour.

2. Add carrots, celery, and onion and continue cooking for 45 minutes.

3. Lift chicken from broth, remove meat from bones and discard skin and bones. Place meat back in broth. Add ½ cup parsley and taste for salt and pepper.

4. Bring to a boil and add Herb Dumplings according to directions.

Serves 10.

Panza llena, corazón contento.

Herb Dumplings

When I make chicken and dumplings I use fresh parsley. For stews, I like to mix some chopped garlic, thyme, and freshly ground black pepper.

2 cups flour
4 teaspoons baking powder
2 teaspoons salt
⅔ cup fresh herbs, chopped (parsley, oregano or thyme)
1 cup milk
4 tablespoons melted butter

1. Sift together flour, baking powder and salt into mixing bowl. Add herbs.

2. Combine milk and melted butter. Add to dry ingredients and stir quickly so dry ingredients are moistened.

3. Drop by tablespoons on top of simmering soup or stew. Cover tightly and simmer 15 minutes.

4. DON'T peek before the time is up. After 15 minutes check for doneness. Cover and cook longer if necessary.

Serves 8.

Full stomach, happy heart.

Chicken Mole

I like to prepare this dish for company. I'm always surprised at how few people know about mole. We really consider it a treat. Serve with a pretty green salad, rice and Crème Brulée (see Index) for dessert! It's a feast!!

6 chicken breast halves
8 chicken thighs
Paprika
3 tablespoons oil (we use canola oil)
1 18-ounce jar mole paste
4 cups water

1. Preheat oven to 350 degrees.
2. Wash and dry chicken pieces. Sprinkle with paprika. Sauté in a hot skillet with oil until chicken is light brown. Remove from pan and place on paper towels to drain off extra grease.
3. Place the chicken in a baking dish. Chicken pieces may be stacked.
4. Empty contents from mole jar into a small mixing bowl. Add water until consistency of thick cream. You may have to add more water depending on how dry the mole mixture is. Pour over chicken.
5. Bake chicken, uncovered, for 1½ hours until chicken is tender. Let rest for 15 minutes.

Serve with rice so you can enjoy the extra gravy!

Serves 10 to 12.

Ni contigo ni sin ti.

Vita's Carne Guisada

Vita, my mother-in-law, was a wonderful cook. She taught me to make this delicious stew soon after I became a Pedregon. My family loves it. When we have leftovers we make carne guisada tacos.

2 pounds round steak, cut into 1" cubes
⅓ cup flour
3 tablespoons canola oil
1 medium onion, chopped
3 to 4 garlic cloves, minced
1 teaspoon salt
1 teaspoon pepper
2 to 3 teaspoons ground comino
2 cups stewed tomatoes, diced
1 cup water

1. Lightly dust meat with flour. Heat oil in a large skillet and brown meat. Add onions and garlic and continue cooking until onions are tender.

2. Add remaining ingredients, and continue cooking, covered, on low heat, for 45 minutes until meat is tender.

Serves 4.

I cannot live with you nor without you.

Italian Meatballs

As an appetizer, wrap in arugula leaves and secure with toothpicks. Arrange on trays and pass them around to your guest's delight. This is one of those fun recipes that people like because of the unusual taste combination!

1 cup coarse **French** bread crumbs
¾ cup milk
2 pounds lean ground beef
1 pound Italian sausage
Zest and juice of 1 lemon
6 garlic cloves, finely chopped
1 cup Parmesan cheese, grated
¼ cup fresh parsley, chopped
2 eggs
1 tablespoon fresh oregano, chopped
1 teaspoon salt
1 teaspoon pepper, freshly ground

1. Preheat oven to 350 degrees.
2. Soak bread crumbs in milk.
3. Measure the remaining ingredients into a large bowl.
4. Squeeze the excess milk out of the bread and add bread to the bowl. Mix the ingredients together until well-combined.
5. Form the meatballs using about 1 tablespoon per meatball for appetizer-size. Use ¼ cup for entrée-size meatballs. Bake on a cookie sheet with raised sides.
6. For appetizer-size meatballs, bake for 15 to 20 minutes. For entrée-size meatballs bake 30 to 40 minutes.

Makes 72 appetizer-size.

Makes 36 entrée-size.

Del plato a la boca a veces se cae la sopa.

Linguini with Smoked Ham-Walnut-Roquefort Sauce

Another of my friend Charles' recipes - elegant and delicious for entertaining. Serve with a salad of field greens with Balsamic Vinaigrette and Tuscan Bread (see Index) and candlelight!

½ pound prosciutto or peppered ham, thinly sliced and shredded
⅓ pound Roquefort cheese or blue cheese, coarsely crumbled
2 cups large walnut pieces, toasted
1 cup Italian parsley, coarsely chopped
¼ cup fresh rosemary, finely chopped
2 garlic cloves, finely minced
1½ teaspoons pepper, freshly ground
1 cup olive oil
1 pound linguini
Freshly grated Parmesan cheese (optional)

1. In a large serving bowl, combine prosciutto or ham, Roquefort or blue cheese, walnuts, parsley, rosemary, garlic, pepper and olive oil. Stir gently and let stand, covered, at room temperature for 4 hours.

2. Cook linguini according to package directions. Drain the pasta and immediately toss with sauce. Serve at once. Top with Parmesan cheese.

Serves 6.

From the plate to the mouth sometimes the soup is spilled.

Sauerbraten

I've had this recipe for years in my recipe file. I don't make it often - but when I do it's really appreciated. It's a great "do ahead" recipe! Serve it with Garlic Mashed Potatoes and Red Cabbage (see Index).

1 cup cider vinegar
1 cup Burgundy
2 onions, quartered
1 carrot sliced
1 stalk celery, chopped
2 whole allspice
4 whole cloves
1 tablespoon salt
1½ teaspoons pepper
4 pounds rump or boned chuck pot roast
4 tablespoons flour
⅓ cup salad oil
1 tablespoon sugar
½ cup gingersnaps, crushed
½ to 1 cup sour cream

1. In large bowl, combine vinegar, Burgundy, onion, carrot, celery, allspice, cloves, salt and pepper.

2. Wipe meat with damp paper towels. Put in marinade - covered for 3 days or longer, turn meat if necessary. Keep refrigerated.

3. Remove meat from marinade. Wipe meat dry. Coat with 2 tablespoons flour.

4. In hot oil in Dutch oven, over medium heat, brown meat well on all sides.

5. Pour in marinade; simmer covered for 2½ to 3 hours or until meat is tender.

6. Remove meat from Dutch oven. Press liquid and vegetables through coarse sieve (another option is to purée the vegetables in the food processor). Skim off fat. Measure 3½ cups liquid (add water, if necessary). Return liquid to Dutch oven.

Viele Köche verderben den Brei.

7. Mix remaining 2 tablespoons flour with ⅓ cup cold water and the sugar. Stir into liquid; bring to boiling, stirring. Stir in gingersnaps and sour cream.

8. Return meat to Dutch oven. Spoon gravy over it; simmer covered 20 minutes.

9. Remove meat to heated platter. Pour some of gravy over it. Serve meat thinly sliced with more gravy.

Serves 6.

Tenderloin

Searing the tenderloin on the grill seals in the flavor and juices - leaving you free to do last minute party preparations while the meat slowly finishes cooking to perfection!

This is Lynda Beal's recipe. Lynda is Helana's mother and she prepares this tenderloin when she entertains. She served it to our family the first time we were invited to the Beal home - it was a perfect day - a wonderful beginning - getting to know our new family!!

1 4 to 5-pound tenderloin
Schilling Montreal Style Steak Seasoning or garlic seasoned
salt and pepper
½ cup butter, melted

1. Sprinkle the entire surface of the tenderloin with seasoning.

2. On grill, brown all sides of tenderloin for 20 to 30 minutes.

3. Brush with butter. Place in preheated 200 degree oven for 1 hour and 30 minutes.

4. Cut in 1" slices and pour juice over meat before serving.

Serves 8 to 10.

Too many cooks are spoiling the broth.

Beef Bourguignon

For entertaining, my thoughts turn to Beef Bourguignon. It's special. I do it in large quantities; and when I'm preparing it, the whole house is filled with a wonderful aroma which lingers until guests arrive. Just add your favorite salad greens tossed with Balsamic Vinaigrette (see Index), crusty bread, Garlic Mashed Potatoes (see Index), a bottle of your favorite red wine and great conversation!!!

½ cup flour
1 teaspoon salt
1 teaspoon pepper
3 to 4 pounds beef chuck, cut in 1½" pieces
5 tablespoons butter
3 tablespoons olive oil
⅓ cup brandy
¼ pound bacon, diced
4 garlic cloves, thinly sliced
3 carrots, cut in ½" diagonals
1 leek, coarsely chopped
½ cup fresh parsley, chopped
2 bay leaves
1 teaspoon thyme
2 cups burgundy wine
1 14½-ounce can beef broth
20 small white onions, 1" in diameter*
1 pound mushrooms, sliced
3 tablespoons butter
Juice of 1 lemon
2 teaspoons sugar
¼ cup parsley, chopped

1. Preheat oven to 350 degrees.
2. Combine flour, salt, and pepper, and dredge meat. In a large, heavy skillet, over high heat, brown meat on all sides in 3 tablespoons butter and oil. This may need to be done in several batches, adding butter and oil if necessary.
3. As meat is browned, place in a large Dutch oven or a large deep roasting pan. When finished with meat browning, add brandy to the skillet to deglaze. Stir and loosen all particles and pour over meat.

4. To the same skillet, add bacon, garlic, carrots, leeks and ¼ cup parsley. Cook, stirring, until bacon and vegetables are lightly browned. Add bay leaves and thyme to skillet, stir, and add bacon mixture to beef. Add wine and enough beef broth to barely cover meat and mix well. Taste for salt and pepper.

5. Cover and bake 1½ hours. Stir occasionally and add more beef broth if necessary.

6. Sauté onions and mushrooms in 3 tablespoons butter until lightly browned. Sprinkle with lemon juice and sugar. Cook for 2 minutes. Add mushrooms and onions to beef and cook 1 more hour, or until beef is tender.

7. Skim any fat and remove bay leaves. Again, taste for salt and pepper. If not serving immediately, refrigerate, removing hardened fat before reheating. When serving, sprinkle with chopped parsley. The Bourguignon freezes beautifully.

Note: The little onions are easy to peel if you place them in boiling water for 1 minute - drain in colander - let cool - and the skins will slip off easily.

Serves 10 to 12.

Chilies Rellenos
(Chilies Stuffed with Cheese)

When we visited Hector's family in El Paso, we were always treated to great Mexican food prepared by our brother-in-law, Manny. What I looked forward to the most were his chilies rellenos. He did it the old fashioned Mexican way and for a time I was so intimidated by the technique that I never thought I could do them myself. Now I've worked out an easier way and we can enjoy them at home anytime!

½ pound Monterey Jack cheese
2 cans peeled green chilies
Flour for coating
6 eggs, separated
6 tablespoons flour
4 to 6 tablespoons oil for frying

1. Cut cheese in rectangles about ½ inch thick and 1 inch long. Wrap a strip of chile around each piece of cheese (each medium-sized chile makes two strips). Roll in flour.
2. Make a batter by beating the whites of eggs until stiff and beating the yolks lightly. Fold yolks into whites, then fold in 2 tablespoons flour.
3. Put 2 tablespoons oil in a large skillet, heat.
4. Pour ⅓ cup batter in the skillet and place on it a chile-wrapped cheese. Fry for a minute or two and then pour just enough batter on top to cover and seal. Fry until its light brown. Slide onto a hot platter and keep warm until ready to serve.

Sauce:
1 tablespoon olive oil
2 cloves garlic, minced
1 medium onion, chopped
1 14½-ounce can tomatoes, chopped, with juice
2 cups chicken broth
1 teaspoon oregano
½ teaspoon pepper
Salt to taste

Las penas con pan son menos.

1. In oil, cook garlic and onion until tender. Add tomatoes. Add remaining ingredients and cook 10 to 15 minutes over medium heat.

2. To serve, heat the chilies in the boiling sauce for about 5 minutes.

Makes 8.

Note: Don't be concerned if the puffy coating deflates. It will puff up again when heated in the sauce.

Hardships are less painful on a full stomach.

Homemade Chorizo

Chorizo is Mexican sausage - generally used at breakfast time scrambled with potatoes and eggs and served on a flour tortilla. Men around these parts love to eat these tacos after an early morning deer hunt. I like to make my own chorizo because I've often been shocked at how greasy some of the commercial ones are. This way I know just what I'm using and I can also vary the amount of chili powder.

1 pound ground pork
1 teaspoon salt
2 tablespoons chili powder
2 garlic cloves, minced
2 tablespoons vinegar

1. Mix all ingredients together thoroughly.
2. Refrigerate several hours or overnight so the flavors can blend.
3. Form into patties (½ cup size and freeze individually so you can use when needed.)

Makes 6.

Six Bar Ranch Sausage

This venison sausage recipe comes from Evelyn Geistweidt, one of our wonderful bakers in the Tea Room. It's a huge amount but this is what she and her family prepare at home when they process deer during hunting season. They put some in pork or beef casings and use the rest as pan sausage. It's a great sausage to have in your freezer for breakfast or to serve with the Braised Cabbage (see Index).

20 pounds meat - (⅔ venison and ⅓ pork or ½ venison and ½ pork)
8 ounces pickling salt
2 ounces pepper, freshly ground - (scant ½ cup)
1 tablespoon salt petre (optional)

1. Grind meat with coarse blade of grinder.
2. Combine all ingredients thoroughly and grind with fine blade.
3. To store, wrap sausage in freezer paper and freeze until needed.

Note: Sprinkle garlic salt in for extra flavor. Salt petre helps keep the meat from turning from pink to grey.

Breads

Garlic Croutons

These are the croutons we use when we make Caesar salad. They are also a very good addition to any of the vegetable soups as a garnish.

¼ cup olive oil
3 to 4 garlic cloves, minced
2 cups French bread, cubed
Romano or Parmesan cheese, grated

1. Preheat oven to 300 degrees.
2. Mix the olive oil with the garlic and sauté with bread cubes until golden.
3. Transfer the croutons to a cookie sheet and sprinkle with cheese.
4. Bake for about 15 minutes or until croutons are crisp.

Makes 2 cups.

Bread Sticks

Use your imagination when doing these delicious bread sticks - roll in fresh cut herbs such as rosemary or brush lightly with honey and sprinkle with cinnamon sugar and crushed anise seed! (Of course, you leave off the salt when you add the sweet).

1 recipe Pizza Dough (see Index)
1 tablespoon olive oil
2 tablespoons coarse sea salt
2 tablespoons pepper, freshly ground

1. Preheat oven to 375 degrees.
2. Divide dough into quarters. Roll out into ½" circumference ropes. Cut into desired lengths. Twist if desired. Lightly brush olive oil on bread sticks with pastry brush. Sprinkle with salt and pepper.
3. Place on sprayed cookie sheet to bake for 10 to 12 minutes, until golden.

Makes 18.

Bread Sticks, Focaccia,
Oatmeal-Raisin Bread, Pesto Butter,
and Tuscan Bread

Salmon and Brie Pizza

Pita Triangles

These taste great in place of chips and make a healthy snack! I serve them with Hummus - they are also good with the Arugula Pesto Torta and the New Year's Black-eyed Pea Spread (see Index).

Pita bread
Olive oil
Jane's Crazy Mixed-Up Salt

1. Preheat oven to 350 degrees.
2. Brush pita bread with olive oil. Cut the bread into small triangular pieces* and arrange them in a single layer on a cookie sheet. Sprinkle with the salt.
3. Bake the triangles for 15 to 20 minutes until lightly toasted.

*Note: Cut into 6 to 12 triangles depending on the size of pita bread you have.

Ottis' Corn Bread

Ottis Layne's corn bread is a recipe that everyone should have in their file. It cooks fast! I make and serve it in my cast iron skillet! A repeat from my first book ... but oh, so necessary!

2 cups white corn meal
¼ cup flour (unbleached or whole wheat)
1 teaspoon salt
2 teaspoons baking powder
¼ teaspoon baking soda
1 egg, beaten
2 cups buttermilk
2 tablespoons butter, melted

1. Preheat oven to 450 degrees.
2. Combine first 5 ingredients in bowl.
3. Combine egg and buttermilk. Add to dry ingredients.
4. Heat butter in oven-proof 10" skillet. Pour batter into sizzling hot skillet. Bake for 20 minutes or until well-browned. Slice into wedges, and serve with butter.

Serves 6 to 8.

Focaccia

I like to serve this bread with pasta dishes, or with a soup and salad meal. It's like a very large tasty homemade cracker!

2 teaspoons active dry yeast
2 teaspoons sugar
¾ cup lukewarm water
2 cups unbleached flour, unsifted
1 teaspoon salt
2 garlic cloves, minced
Olive oil
Parmesan, grated
3 tablespoons fresh rosemary or oregano, chopped

1. Dissolve yeast and sugar in lukewarm water.

2. Combine flour and salt. Add to the yeast mixture, stirring well with wooden spoon. (This step can also be done in a food processor using a dough blade.)

3. Knead the dough on a slightly floured board until it is no longer sticky. Place the dough in an oiled bowl; brush top of dough with oil also. Cover, and let rise until doubled, about one hour.

4. After dough has doubled in size, punch it down and turn onto floured board. Divide into 2 parts. Pat dough into 2 circles (about 7" each). Brush dough with olive oil and sprinkle Parmesan cheese and herbs on top. Make decorative slits in the dough. Let dough rise for 15 minutes.

5. Bake in a preheated 400 degree oven for 20 minutes.

Serves 8 to 10.

Wie die Backen so die Hacken.

Dried Cranberry Scones

Another special tea time delight from my friend, Sally. Plan to enjoy them fresh from the oven!

1 teaspoon cinnamon
4 tablespoons honey
½ cup dried cranberries
Peel from 1 lemon
2 tablespoons lemon juice
2 cups unbleached flour
½ teaspoon baking soda
2 teaspoons baking powder
Pinch salt
¼ cup unsalted butter
½ cup buttermilk or plain yogurt

1. Preheat oven to 425 degrees.
2. Combine cinnamon, honey, dried cranberries, lemon peel and juice and let soak for 30 minutes to an hour.
3. Mix flour, soda, baking powder and salt. Cut butter into dry ingredients until it resembles fine crumbs.
4. Add buttermilk or yogurt and mix until thoroughly moistened.
5. On floured board roll out dough to ½". Cut into triangles. Place on greased baking sheets and bake 12 to 15 minutes, until light brown.

Orange Currant Scones
Follow Dried Cranberry Scones recipe and leave out dried cranberries, lemon juice and peel. Add peel from 1 orange, juice of ½ orange, ½ cup currants and decrease honey to 3 tablespoons.

Makes 12.

The way a man chews his food shows how he will work — slow or fast.

Apricot Streusel Muffins

These muffins are nice and light. Vary the recipe with peach or strawberry preserves.

1¾ cups all-purpose flour
¼ cup light brown sugar
2½ teaspoons baking powder
½ teaspoon salt
1 egg, beaten
¾ cup milk
⅓ cup cooking oil
½ cup apricot preserves

1. Preheat oven to 400 degrees.
2. Grease 2½" muffin cups or line with paper bake cups. Set aside.
3. In a medium mixing bowl, stir together flour, sugar, baking powder and salt. Make a well in the center.
4. In a small mixing bowl, combine egg, milk and oil. Add egg mixture all at once to flour mixture stirring just till moistened. Batter should be slightly lumpy. Spoon about 1 tablespoon batter into each prepared cup. Add about 1 teaspoon apricot preserves. Spoon another tablespoon batter over preserves in each cup.

Topping:
2 tablespoons flour
2 tablespoons brown sugar
1 tablespoon butter, softened
1 teaspoon cinnamon
½ teaspoon nutmeg
2 tablespoons walnuts, chopped

1. In a small bowl combine flour, brown sugar, butter, ground cinnamon and nutmeg. Stir in chopped nuts. Sprinkle over batter in muffin cups.
2. Bake in preheated oven for 15 to 20 minutes or till golden. Remove from pans and serve hot.

Makes 12 muffins.

Corn Muffins

Corn muffins at their very best - the extra addition of corn makes them moist and flavorful!

1 cup corn meal
1 cup unbleached white flour
¼ cup sugar
2½ teaspoons baking powder
¼ teaspoon salt
1 cup buttermilk or yogurt
8 tablespoons butter, melted
1 egg, slightly beaten
1 cup corn, chopped
½ cup pimentos, sliced

1. Preheat oven to 400 degrees.
2. Measure the corn meal, flour, sugar, baking powder, and salt into a mixing bowl. Make a well in the center and pour in the buttermilk or yogurt, butter and egg. Stir only until combined.
3. Fold in the corn and pimentos.
4. Fill each greased muffin cup with batter. Bake until firm and golden, 20 to 25 minutes.

Makes 12 muffins

Blueberry-Pecan Corn Muffins

I love these corn muffins. I particularly like the flavors of the corn-blueberry-pecan combination. We have also done these with chopped red peppers added and they were scrumptious! It's fun for entertaining because it's a surprise for your guests!

1 cup corn meal
1 cup unbleached white flour
¼ cup sugar
2½ teaspoons baking powder
¼ teaspoon salt
1 cup buttermilk or yogurt
8 tablespoons butter, melted
1 egg, slightly beaten
1½ cups blueberries
1 cup toasted pecans, chopped

1. Preheat oven to 400 degrees.
2. Measure the corn meal, flour, sugar, baking powder, and salt into a mixing bowl. Make a well in the center and pour in the buttermilk or yogurt, butter and egg. Stir only until combined.
3. Fold in the blueberries and pecans just until combined.
4. Fill each greased muffin cup two-thirds full with batter. Bake until firm and golden, 20 to 25 minutes.

Makes 12 muffins.

Con hambre no hay mal pan.

Taos Corn Muffins

A great addition to a meal when serving Southwestern food.

1 cup corn meal
1 cup unbleached white flour
¼ cup sugar
2½ teaspoons baking powder
¼ teaspoon salt
1 cup buttermilk or yogurt
8 tablespoons butter, melted
1 egg, slightly beaten
1 cup corn, chopped
½ cup pimentos, sliced
¼ cup jalapeños or ½ cup green chilies

1. Preheat oven to 400 degrees.
2. Measure the corn meal, flour, sugar, baking powder, and salt into a mixing bowl. Make a well in the center and pour in the buttermilk or yogurt, butter and egg. Stir only until combined.
3. Fold in the corn, pimentos and jalapeños or chilies.
4. Fill each greased muffin cup with batter. Bake until firm and golden, 20 to 25 minutes.

Makes 12 muffins.

The hungry man thinks all food was well prepared.

Tuscan Bread

I love to make - and eat - this wonderful classic peasant bread. It's crusty on the outside, and moist and tender inside. Serve it, as the Italians do, next to a saucer of Lemon Olive Oil (see Index).

There are many variations to try. I've listed several of my successes below - try these, and then let your imagination go!

3 cups water
1½ tablespoons active dry yeast
2 teaspoons sugar
6 to 8 cups unbleached white flour
1 tablespoon salt

1. In a large bowl, combine water, yeast, sugar and 3 cups flour. Mix well and cover with plastic wrap. Let set for at least 2 to 3 hours, or overnight, until a spongy dough forms.

2. Add salt and remaining flour, a cup at a time and mix well until a soft dough is formed.

3. Turn onto a floured board and knead well for 5 to 10 minutes until smooth and elastic, adding a little more flour if necessary to prevent sticking.

4. Place dough in bowl and cover again with plastic wrap (this is important, because there is no oil in this bread to prevent a dry crust forming on the dough's surface). Let rise until doubled, about 1 hour.

5. Punch dough down, shape into 2 round loaves and place on a greased cookie sheet that has been sprinkled with corn meal. Let rise until doubled, about 30 to 45 minutes.

6. Using a serrated knife, make shallow diagonal slashes on top of loaf. Bake in a preheated 400 degree oven for 30 minutes.

Makes 2 loaves.

Note: Because this is a wonderful classic, crusty bread, I often add one of the following variations. Add the ingredients at the end of the second step.

La fe mueve montañas.

Variations:

1. Add ½ cup toasted walnuts, ½ cup sun-dried tomatoes, chopped; or

2. Add ½ cup toasted almonds and dried cherries, or cranberries.

3. Add ½ cup dried apricots, chopped and ½ cup pine nuts, toasted lightly; or

4. Add ¾ cup golden raisins, ½ cup pine nuts, toasted lightly.

Olive Walnut Bread

I like to make this unusual quick bread when we do snack buffets. It also makes a nice gift when presented with a small crock of goat cheese.

2 eggs
2 tablespoons olive oil
¾ cup green olives with pimentos, coarsely chopped
¾ cup pitted black olives, coarsely chopped
½ cup walnuts, toasted and chopped
1½ cups unbleached wheat flour
½ cup whole wheat flour
2 teaspoons sugar
1 tablespoon baking powder
½ teaspoon salt
1 teaspoon pepper, freshly ground
½ cup milk

1. Preheat oven to 350 degrees.

2. In a mixing bowl, mix together eggs, olive oil, olives, and walnuts. Mix well.

3. Combine flours, sugar, baking powder, salt, and pepper. Stir into creamed mixture alternately with the milk.

4. Pour into a buttered loaf pan. Bake for 45 to 50 minutes.

5. Remove from oven, let rest in pan for 10 minutes, invert on rack and let cool before slicing.

Makes 1 loaf.

Faith moves mountains.

"Super Good for You" Whole Wheat Bread

A bread packed with nutrition! It makes a very pretty loaf and a delicious sandwich bread. Note: The only oil in this bread is in the oiled bowl and the little bit that you brush on the loaves.

3 cups whole wheat flour, divided
2 tablespoon yeast
1½ cups water
½ cup sorghum syrup, molasses or honey
½ cup sunflower seeds, coarsely chopped
½ cup pumpkin seeds, coarsely chopped
½ cup walnuts, coarsely chopped
¼ cup flax seeds
½ cup raisins
1 tablespoon salt
1 cup oats
2 cups milk, scalded and cooled
3 to 4 cups unbleached white flour
Oil
Melted butter

1. In a large bowl, combine 1½ cups whole wheat flour, yeast, water and sorghum syrup, molasses or honey. Mix well and cover with plastic wrap. Let set for at least 2 to 3 hours, or overnight, until a spongy dough forms. Do not refrigerate.

2. Combine seeds, raisins, salt, oats and milk. Add to flour-yeast mixture and mix well.

3. Add the unbleached flour and the remaining whole wheat flour. Mix well and turn onto floured board. Knead for 10 minutes until smooth and elastic, adding more flour as needed to prevent sticking.*

4. Form dough into large ball. Place dough in oiled bowl and brush the top with oil. Cover with towel and let rise until doubled in size, about 1 hour.

5. Turn onto floured board. Divide dough into 2 parts, form into loaves, and place each in greased bread pan. Let rise again until doubled, about 30 to 45 minutes.

6. Bake in preheated 375 degree oven for 40 to 45 minutes until golden brown. Remove from pans and cool on wire rack. While cooling, brush tops with melted butter.

Makes 2 large loaves.

Note: Whole grains take longer to absorb liquid, so take care to add flour just as needed.

Walnut French Bread

This is a delicious loaf for sandwiches. I also bake this in heart-shaped bread pans for the Tea Room - it makes 2 heart loaves.

¾ cup warm water
1 tablespoon yeast
2 teaspoons sugar
3½ cups flour
¼ cup walnut oil
1 egg
½ cup walnuts, toasted and chopped
2 teaspoons salt

1. Place all ingredients in food processor.
2. Process until dough forms a ball and cleans sides of bowl. If it seems sticky, let it rest for 2 to 3 minutes before turning on the motor again. Process until dough forms ball and cleans sides of bowl.
3. Place in mixing bowl and let rise until doubled, about 1 hour.
4. Turn dough onto lightly floured board, form into loaf and place in a lightly greased bread pan. Let rise again until doubled, about 30 to 45 minutes.
5. Bake in preheated oven at 375 degrees for about 45 to 50 minutes.

Makes 1 loaf.

Garlic Potato Bread

Using potatoes in bread makes for a light flavorful loaf. This one is enhanced by the addition of garlic - if you have Roasted Garlic (see Index) stored in your freezer, use it in this recipe.

2 tablespoons active dry yeast
2 tablespoons honey
1½ cups lukewarm water
2 cups potatoes, mashed
1 tablespoon salt
½ cup butter, softened
1 tablespoon garlic, minced
2 cups whole wheat flour
3 cups unbleached white flour

1. Mix the yeast and honey into the lukewarm water. Let it dissolve until bubbly.

2. Combine the potato, salt, butter and garlic and stir well. Add the yeast mixture and stir well. (This step can also be done in a food processor using a dough blade.)

3. Add the flours and beat well until the dough is smooth. (If you do this in the food processor, the dough will not need to be kneaded by hand.)

4. Knead the dough on a slightly floured board until it is no longer sticky. Place the dough in an oiled bowl; brush top of dough with oil. Cover and let rise until doubled, about 1 to 2 hours depending on how warm your kitchen is.

5. Punch dough down and turn onto floured board. Divide dough into 2 parts, form into loaves, and place each in greased bread pan. Let rise again until doubled, about 30 to 40 minutes.

6. Bake in preheated 375 degree oven for 40 to 45 minutes until golden brown. Remove from pans and cool on wire rack. While cooling, brush tops with melted butter.

Makes 2 large loaves.

Primero cae un hablador que un cojo.

Garlic-Jalapeño-Potato Bread

A spectacular loaf of bread - tender, light, moist and delicious. For a variation, when forming the loaves, add ½ cup grated cheese to each loaf - Monterey Jack or Cheddar are both great!

2 tablespoons active dry yeast
2 tablespoons honey
1½ cups lukewarm water
2 cups potatoes, cooked, mashed
½ cup milk, scalded and cooled
2 eggs
1 tablespoon salt
½ cup butter, softened
2 teaspoons garlic
1 cup oats
⅓ cup jalapeños, chopped
2 cups whole wheat flour
4 to 5 cups unbleached white flour

1. Mix the yeast and honey into the lukewarm water. Let it dissolve until bubbly.

2. Combine the potatoes, milk, eggs, salt, butter, garlic and oats and stir well. Add the yeast mixture and jalapeños and stir well. (This step can also be done in a food processor using a dough blade.)

3. Add the flours and beat well until the dough is smooth. (If you do this in the food processor the dough will not need to be kneaded by hand.)

4. Knead the dough on a slightly floured board until it is no longer sticky. Place the dough in an oiled bowl; brush top of dough with oil. Cover and let rise until doubled, about 1 to 2 hours depending on how warm your kitchen is.

5. Punch dough down and turn onto floured board. Divide dough into 3 parts, form into loaves, and place each in greased bread pan. Let rise again until doubled, about 30 to 40 minutes.

6. Bake in preheated 375 degree oven for 40 to 45 minutes until golden brown. Remove from pans and cool on wire rack. While cooling, brush tops with melted butter.

Makes 3 loaves.

A gossiper will fall quicker than a cripple.

Cottage-Cheese Onion Dill Bread

Truly this is a wonderful bread for your collection - adding cottage cheese creates a very light bread and the addition of onion and dill gives each bite a flavor explosion! It makes two very large and beautifully fragrant loaves.

3 tablespoons yeast
3 tablespoons honey
1 cup warm water
3 cups cottage cheese
1 teaspoon salt
1 teaspoon soda
½ cup butter, softened
3 large eggs
1 package onion soup mix
½ cup fresh dill weed, or 3 tablespoons dried
1 teaspoon pepper
2 cups whole wheat flour
6 to 8 cups unbleached flour

1. Add yeast and honey to warm water, stir until dissolved.

2. In a large bowl combine cottage cheese, salt, soda, butter, eggs, soup mix, dill and pepper. Mix well.

3. Add the yeast mixture and the whole wheat flour, and mix well.

4. Add the remaining flour, 2 cups at a time, to make a stiff dough.

5. Turn onto a lightly floured bread board and knead thoroughly until dough is smooth and elastic.

6. Place dough in a clean bowl, cover, and let rise until doubled.

7. Turn onto a lightly floured bread board again and knead lightly. Divide dough into 2 parts and shape into loaves and place in buttered loaf pans. Cover and let rise until doubled.

8. Bake in a preheated 350 degree oven about 40 to 45 minutes.

Makes 2 large loaves.

Orange Bow-Knot Rolls

Bow-knot rolls are a delicious and very festive addition to any meal - but especially for the holidays. In my friend Sally Layne's family they have been a Thanksgiving and Christmas tradition for 50 years.

1¼ cups milk, scalded
½ cup shortening
⅓ cup sugar
1 teaspoon salt
1 cake fresh yeast
2 eggs, beaten
¼ cup orange juice
2 tablespoons orange zest, grated
5 cups flour

1. Combine hot milk, shortening, sugar and salt. Cool to lukewarm. Add yeast to this mixture and let soften.

2. Add eggs, orange juice, orange zest and beat thoroughly.

3. Add flour. Mix to form a soft dough. Cover and let stand 10 minutes.

4. Knead on lightly floured surface. Place in oiled bowl and let rise until double in size (about 2 hours).

5. Punch down and roll dough to ½" thick. Cut into 10" x ¾" strips. To form the bows, pinch off a 2" piece from each 10" strip. Fold the resulting 8" strip to look like a bow. Use the 2" strip to make a knot and tie.

6. Arrange on a greased sheet. Cover and let rise until doubled.

7. Bake in preheated oven at 400 degrees for 15 minutes. Spread with orange topping while still warm.

Orange Topping:
2 tablespoons orange juice
1 teaspoon orange peel, grated
1 cup powdered sugar, sifted

Mix all ingredients thoroughly to a glaze consistency.

Makes 24.

Oatmeal Raisin Bread

Delicious anytime - a real treat toasted for breakfast!!

4 cups scalded milk
2 cups old fashioned oats
¼ cup butter
½ cup molasses or honey
1 tablespoon salt
2 tablespoons yeast
¼ cup warm water
2 cups whole wheat flour
8 cups flour
1 cup raisins or currants
1 cup pecans, coarsely chopped

1. Pour hot milk over the oats, butter, molasses or honey and salt and let set for 20 minutes.

2. Dissolve yeast in warm water.

3. Add dissolved yeast to cooled milk mixture. Add whole wheat flour and mix well.

4. Add the remaining flour, 2 cups at a time, to make a soft dough. Knead until smooth and elastic. Add nuts and currants or raisins and knead into dough. Place dough in buttered bowl. Cover and let rise until doubled.

5. Turn onto a lightly floured bread board again and knead lightly. Divide dough into 3 loaves and place in buttered loaf pans. Let rise until doubled.

6. Bake in a preheated 400 degree oven for 45 to 50 minutes. Butter tops of loaves while it's still hot.

Makes 3 loaves.

Note: This is a very versatile recipe - substitute dried cherries or cranberries for the raisins - and use sunflower seeds, almonds or peanuts in place of - or mixed with the pecans!

Christmas Stollen

Stollen has the best flavor after 2 to 3 days. If you're giving it for gifts - sprinkle on more powdered sugar - then wrap and add a pretty bow!

2 cups milk, scalded and cooled
1 tablespoon sugar
1 tablespoon salt
10 to 12 cups flour
2 tablespoons yeast, dissolved in ¼ cup warm water
1 pound butter
1½ cups sugar
6 eggs
⅓ cup brandy
Zest of 1 lemon
2 cups almonds, slivered
2 cups golden raisins or currants
Melted butter
Powdered sugar

1. In a large bowl, combine milk, sugar, salt, 2 cups flour and dissolved yeast. Mix well and cover with plastic wrap. Let set for about 2 hours, until a spongy dough forms. Do not refrigerate.

2. In a separate bowl, cream the butter and sugar until fluffy. Add eggs, brandy, and lemon zest. Mix well.

3. Stir in 5 cups flour, then add the yeast mixture, mixing well. Add the remaining flour 1 cup at a time until a stiff dough is formed. Stir in the almonds and raisins or currents.

4. Turn dough onto a floured board. Knead for 10 minutes until smooth and elastic.

5. Form dough into a large ball. Place in oiled bowl and turn ball of dough to coat with oil. Cover with a towel and let rise until doubled in size, about 1 hour.

6. Turn onto floured board. Divide dough into 3 parts and shape into an oval. Fold oval over so that it gives you the traditional stollen shape. Place on buttered cookie sheet and let rise until doubled. Brush with melted butter. Bake in preheated 350 degree oven for 1 hour to 1 hour and 15 minutes, until golden.

7. While loaves are still hot, brush with melted butter. Sprinkle liberally with powdered sugar and let cool.

Makes 3 loaves.

Notes

Pizza Dough

"This is the basic pizza dough recipe. You may make variations on it by using chopped herbs in the crust. I like to sprinkle chopped rosemary, sea salt and olive oil around the rim of the crust just before baking - this makes a softer crust." -- Tina

1 teaspoon sugar
1 cup warm water
1 tablespoon yeast
3 cups flour
1 teaspoon salt
¼ cup olive oil
1 tablespoon olive oil

1. In a measuring cup, lightly stir the sugar, water and yeast and set aside to rise.

2. Measure the flour and salt into food processor and blend. Slowly pour in yeast mixture and then ¼ cup olive oil. Mix until dough just forms a fall. Avoid overworking the dough.

3. Pour about a tablespoon of olive oil into a large mixing bowl. Gather the pizza dough to form into a ball. Turn dough until it's coated with olive oil. Cover and let the dough rise for 1 hour and 30 minutes. If you are unable to use the pizza dough immediately, you may punch the dough down and turn it over to rise up to a total of four times.

4. To shape the pizza dough into a 12" round, place a ball of dough on a lightly floured surface and dust the top of the dough lightly with flour. Using the heels of your hands, press the dough into a circle.

Makes 1 crust.

Corn Meal Pizza Dough

1. Instead of 3 cups flour, use 2 cups flour and 1 cup yellow corn meal.

2. Follow Pizza Dough recipe instructions.

Note: Brushing the crust with olive oil **before** baking creates a softer crust. Brushing the rim of the crust **after** baking makes the pizza crust shine beautifully!

Tina's Italian Pizza Sauce

Tina uses this sauce as a basic when she is baking pizza. Use a little less when making pizzas with mild ingredients and a little more when making heartier pizzas. It is also fine to add hot Italian sausage or lean ground beef to the sauce during the first step.

4 garlic cloves, minced
1 medium onion, chopped
¼ cup olive oil
2 28-ounce cans Italian-style whole tomatoes, chopped, with juice
2 teaspoons sugar
2 teaspoons salt
2 teaspoons dried basil
1 bay leaf
1 teaspoon pepper, freshly ground

1. Sauté the garlic and onion in the olive oil until the onions are soft and transparent.

2. Add the rest of the ingredients and bring the sauce to a boil. Turn down the heat to simmer for one hour.

Sauce for two 12" pizzas.

Salmon and Brie Pizza

The classic appetizer twosome of salmon and Brie is an interesting combination for a pizza. Make this for dinner or slice small for an appetizer. Be sure to serve with a bottle of good red wine.

2 cups Tina's Italian Pizza Sauce (see previous page)
1 recipe Pizza Dough (see Index)
¾ to 1 pound salmon fillet, uncooked, deboned and sliced
½ pound Brie with the white coating sliced off
10 thin slices yellow bell pepper
5 thin slices red onion
Garnish: Fresh basil sprig

1. Preheat oven to 500 degrees.
2. Spread sauce evenly over dough. Arrange the salmon, Brie, yellow pepper slices and red onion slices over the sauce.
3. Bake for 20 to 25 minutes until the crust in golden. Garnish with a fresh basil sprig.

Serves 6 to 8.

Note: There are several different kinds of Brie that you may use. Coeur de Brie is probably the easiest to handle since it has no rind on the sides.

David's Salmon Pizza

Tina's friend, David, helped create this pizza. She offered to bake a pizza for him if he would bring something to put on it - he appeared with a beautiful salmon fillet and this great new pizza was born.

2 cups Tina's Italian Pizza Sauce (see Index)
1 recipe Pizza Dough (see Index)
2 cups mozzarella or Provolone cheese, grated
2 ounces herb goat cheese
1 pound uncooked salmon fillet, deboned and sliced

1. Preheat oven to 450 degrees.
2. Spread sauce evenly over dough. Sprinkle cheeses over sauce. Arrange salmon slices on top.
3. Bake for 20 to 30 minutes.

Serves 6 to 8.

Shrimp Pizza

Use jumbo shrimp for a great impression - the size and color are beautiful.

3 cups Tina's Italian Pizza Sauce (see Index)
1 recipe Pizza Dough (see Index)
1 pound jumbo or medium sized shrimp, shelled, uncooked
2½ cups Lappi cheese, shredded
2 ounces herb goat cheese
1 tablespoon chopped fresh basil or 1 teaspoon dried

1. Preheat oven to 500 degrees.
2. Spread sauce evenly over dough. Arrange shrimp and sprinkle both cheeses on top. Sprinkle basil on top.
3. Bake for 20 to 25 minutes until the crust is golden.

Serves 6 to 8.

Note: Mozzarella or Provolone can be substituted for Lappi cheese. Lappi cheese is a smooth cheese that goes well with seafood.

Summer Alfresco Pizza

A hearty pizza that will entice you with it's different colors from fresh summer produce. It is well worth the search for yellow tomatoes and purple bell peppers to make this pizza.

5 cups Tina's Italian Pizza Sauce (see Index)
1 recipe Pizza Dough (see Index)
½ pound Hot Italian Sausage, cooked and sliced into chunks
½ pound mozzarella cheese , shredded
¼ pound Provolone cheese, shredded or sliced
6 thin slices red tomato
8 thin slices yellow tomato
8 thin slices orange bell pepper
8 thin slices purple bell pepper
2 ounces plain goat cheese
1 tablespoon fresh oregano, chopped or 1 teaspoon dried
1 tablespoon fresh basil, chopped or 1 teaspoon dried

1. Preheat oven to 500 degrees.
2. Spread sauce evenly over dough. Arrange layers of sausage, mozzarella, Provolone, tomatoes, peppers, goat cheese. Top with oregano and basil.
3. Bake for 20 to 25 minutes or until crust is golden.

Serves 6 to 8.

Canadian Bacon Pizza

Very light - and very tasty!

3 cups Tina's Italian Pizza Sauce (see Index)
1 recipe Pizza Dough (see Index)
1 pound Canadian bacon, uncooked and sliced
½ pound Muenster cheese, thinly sliced
Pepper, freshly ground

1. Preheat oven to 500 degrees.
2. Spread sauce evenly over dough. Arrange Canadian bacon and cheese over sauce. Grind pepper over cheese.
3. Bake for 20 to 25 minutes until the crust is golden.

Serves 6 to 8.

Helana's Simple BBQ Chicken Pizza

Helana made this for my surprise birthday party -- it's David's favorite kind of pizza. It's very simple to do and your family or guests will love it!

1 pound chicken breasts, sliced
1 cup prepared barbecue sauce (Kraft Thick n' Spicy Honey)
1 recipe Pizza Dough (see Index)
½ pound mozzarella cheese, shredded

1. Preheat oven to 400 degrees.
2. Cook chicken breasts in a covered dish in barbecue sauce for 10 minutes. Slice cooked chicken into bite size pieces.
3. Spread barbecue sauce and chicken evenly over dough. Top with cheese.
4. Bake for 20 to 25 minutes.

Serves 6 to 8.

Country Chicken Pizza

Tina likes to make this pizza with barbecue Chicken strips because of the good flavor they add - roasted chicken works well, too.

2 cups Tina's Italian Pizza Sauce (see Index)
1 recipe Pizza Dough (see Index)
2 cups barbecue or roasted chicken cut in strips (without barbecue sauce)
2 cups farmers cheese, grated
12 thin slices red bell pepper
8 thin slices red onion
Pepper, freshly ground, to taste

1. Preheat oven to 500 degrees.
2. Spread sauce evenly over dough.
3. Place chicken and cheeses on sauce. Arrange bell pepper and onion slices on pizza. Top with freshly ground pepper.
4. Bake for 20 to 25 minutes.

Serves 6 to 8

Roasted Eggplant and Rosemary Pizza

When Tina is making pizzas in our kitchen, word spreads so fast it quickly becomes party-time at the Pedregon's. It's easy calling friends on the spur of the moment - this invitation is readily accepted.

4 slices baked eggplant, ¼" thick slices
Salt and pepper
6 thin slices prosciutto
1 recipe Pizza Dough (see Index)
3 cups Tina's Italian Pizza Sauce (see Index)
1 cup hot Italian Sausage, sliced
8 thin slices red bell pepper
2 cups mozzarella cheese, grated
2 ounces goat cheese
Olive oil
Coarse sea salt
Fresh rosemary

1. Preheat oven to 375 degrees.
2. Place the eggplant on a cookie sheet. Brush with olive oil and sprinkle with salt and pepper. Bake for 20 minutes until golden.
3. Preheat oven to 500 degrees.
4. Place prosciutto on dough then spread on sauce. Next arrange eggplant on pizza and follow with sausage, pepper slices, mozzarella and goat cheeses.
5. Brush olive oil on the rim of the crust, sprinkle with a light amount of coarse sea salt and rosemary.
6. Bake for 20 to 25 minutes until crust is golden.

Serves 6 to 8.

Eggplant and Prosciutto Pizza

Tina really knows how to make pizza special. This one is unique because of the corn meal crust - it's slightly crunchy. The flavors of eggplant, prosciutto and sautéed garlic blend well.

6 ¼" slices eggplant, baked and quartered
Olive oil
Salt and pepper to taste
3 garlic cloves, sliced
2 tablespoons olive oil
1 Corn Meal Pizza Dough (see Index)
2 cups Tina's Italian Pizza Sauce (see Index)
5 slices prosciutto
1 cup Provolone cheese, sliced
1 cup mozzarella cheese, grated
2 ounces herb goat cheese
Pepper, freshly ground

1. Preheat oven to 375 degrees.
2. Place the eggplant slices on a cookie sheet and brush with olive oil. Sprinkle with salt and pepper. Bake for 20 minutes. Set aside.
3. Sauté garlic in olive oil and set aside.
4. Preheat oven to 500 degrees.
5. On dough, layer sauce, prosciutto, eggplant, Provolone, mozzarella, herb goat cheese, garlic and pepper.
6. Bake for 20 to 30 minutes until the crust is golden and the cheese has melted.

Serves 6 to 8.

Tomatillo y Pollo Pizza

If you want to know what this pizza is like, imagine what happens when you put together the passion of the Italians with the fire of the Mexicans!!!

3 cups Tomatillo Pizza Sauce (recipe following)
1 recipe Pizza Dough (see Index)
3 cups barbecue chicken, sliced
2 cups green chilies, thinly sliced
3 cups Monterey Jack cheese, shredded
2 ounces plain goat cheese
1 tablespoon chopped jalapeños, or to taste
⅓ cup black olives, cut in half
Garnish: Cilantro sprigs

1. Preheat oven to 500 degrees.
2. Spread sauce evenly over dough. Arrange chicken and green chilies on dough. Next sprinkle on cheeses and jalapeños. Top with black olives.
3. Bake for 20 to 25 minutes until the crust in golden. Garnish with cilantro sprigs.

Tomatillo Pizza Sauce

2 pounds tomatillos, husks removed
1 small onion, chopped
2 garlic cloves, minced
2 tablespoons olive oil
1 teaspoon salt
2 tablespoons cilantro, finely chopped

1. Place tomatillos in boiling salted water for about 3 minutes. Drain and coarsely chop.
2. In skillet, sauté onion and garlic in olive oil. Add tomatillos, salt and cilantro. Bring to a boil and then lower heat and continue cooking for 30 minutes.

Makes 4 cups.

Cakes

Lemon Balm Cake

Lemon Balm is one of the more prolific plants in my garden - its leaves are lemon scented. I especially enjoy their fragrance when I'm watering my garden. This cake is especially good at teatime.

1 cup mixed lemon verbena and lemon balm leaves, rinsed, dried and finely chopped
1 cup butter or margarine, softened
1¾ cups sugar
6 egg whites
3 cups sifted white flour
4 teaspoons baking powder
½ teaspoon salt
¾ cup milk
½ cup water
1 teaspoon vanilla

1. Preheat oven to 350 degrees.
2. Using the electric mixer, cream chopped leaves with butter or margarine and add sugar gradually until light and fluffy. Add egg whites 2 at a time, beating well after each addition.
3. Sift together flour, baking powder and salt.
4. Combine milk, water and vanilla.
5. Alternately add dry ingredients and milk mixture to creamed mixture, beginning and ending with dry ingredients. Beat smooth after each addition.
6. Pour batter into 2 greased and floured 9" cake pans.
7. Bake for 25 to 30 minutes, or until done.
8. Cool in pans for 10 minutes - remove from pans. Frost when cooled.

Lemon Frosting:
¾ cup butter, softened
Juice from 2 lemons
Zest of 1 lemon
3 tablespoons milk
6 cups powdered sugar
Garnish: Lemon verbena leaves (lemon balm is pretty but wilts very quickly). Lemon geranium would be good, too.

1. Using an electric mixer or food processor, cream butter. Add lemon juice, lemon zest and milk. Gradually add powdered sugar.

Serves 12 to 14.

Chocolate Pound Cake

The only way to improve a pound cake is to make it chocolate!

1 cup boiling water
2 squares unsweetened baking chocolate
2 cups flour
1 teaspoon baking soda
¼ teaspoon salt
½ cup butter or margarine
1¾ cups brown sugar, packed
2 eggs
1 teaspoon vanilla
½ cup sour cream or buttermilk

1. Preheat oven to 325 degrees.
2. Pour boiling water into a small bowl and melt the chocolate in it. Set aside. Grease a 9" x 5" x 3" bread pan.
3. In another bowl, measure flour, soda and salt. In a larger bowl, using an electric mixer, cream the butter or margarine with the sugar, eggs and vanilla until light. Alternate adding the flour mixture with the sour cream or buttermilk, blending well, and then beat in the cooled chocolate-water mixture.
4. Pour the batter into the greased and floured loaf pan and bake for about 1 hour until the cake has risen and is lightly browned.
5. Remove the cake from the oven and cool for 15 minutes. Remove from pan and let cool on rack.

Chocolate Glaze:
½ cup powdered sugar
¼ cup cocoa
2 tablespoons milk
¼ teaspoon vanilla

Mix all ingredients until smooth and creamy. Drizzle on cake.

Makes 1 loaf.

Elena's Cake

We have a very special group of friends who meet for food and fellowship. This is the cake that my friend Elena brings - it's so special having friends you can depend on for friendship and support ... and buttermilk cake too!

1 cup Crisco
½ cup butter
2½ cups sugar
5 eggs
½ teaspoon soda
2 tablespoons hot water
3 cups flour
1 cup buttermilk
1 teaspoon almond extract

1. Preheat oven to 350 degrees.

2. Cream together Crisco and butter with sugar in mixer.

3. Add eggs one at a time - continuing to beat. Add soda dissolved with hot water.

4. Alternately add flour and milk.

5. Lower speed and add soda mixed with extract.

6. Pour in greased and floured tube pan. Bake for 1 hour and 15 to 20 minutes.

7. Remove from oven. After 10 minutes remove from pan. Glaze while it's still warm. (Pierce with a toothpick for glaze to penetrate cake.)

Coffee Glaze:
3 tablespoons butter, softened
Dash salt
2 tablespoons milk
¾ teaspoon vanilla
1 teaspoon instant coffee dissolved in a little hot water
½ cup powdered sugar

Place all ingredients except powdered sugar in a measuring cup and microwave until butter is melted. Add powdered sugar. Mix thoroughly.

Serves 12 to 14.

Bride Helana
1994 ♡

White Chocolate Brownie Cheesecake
with Raspberry Sauce
and Carlos' Eggnog

Lemon Balm Cake

Chocolate Walnut Cakes

These little cakes are rich and delicious - good for any occasion - a special treat for sack lunches.

2 cups flour
⅓ cup sugar
⅓ cup brown sugar
½ teaspoon salt
2 teaspoons baking powder
2 eggs
⅔ cup milk
1½ teaspoons vanilla
½ cup butter, melted
2 cups chocolate chips
½ cup walnuts

1. Preheat the oven to 400 degrees.

2. Mix together the flour with the sugars, salt and baking powder and set aside.

3. In a separate bowl, beat the eggs with the milk, vanilla and butter.

4. Fold the dry ingredients into the egg and butter mixture. Add the chocolate chips and the walnuts but only mix enough to combine.

5. Grease 12 regular size muffin cups and spoon the batter into the tins. Bake the cakes for 15 to 20 minutes until a toothpick comes out clean.

6. Let the cakes cool in pans before taking them out. The chocolate chips tend to stick to the pans if they are taken out while they are hot.

Makes 12 cakes.

Collins Chocolate Cake

*No cookbook of mine would ever be complete without this chocolate cake recipe.
I included it in* The Peach Tree Tea Room *cookbook and also in this one because I
want to make sure it never gets overlooked. This is the best cake that I've ever tasted
- it's been in my family for many years. Enjoy - Enjoy!!*

4 ounces unsweetened baking chocolate
1 cup butter or margarine
1 cup brewed coffee
2 cups sugar
⅔ cup buttermilk
1 teaspoon baking soda
2 eggs
½ teaspoon cinnamon
2 teaspoons vanilla
2 cups flour

1. Preheat oven to 350 degrees.
2. In a large saucepan, combine chocolate, butter or margarine, and coffee. Heat, stirring constantly, until chocolate and butter are melted. Add sugar and continue cooking over low heat until sugar is dissolved.
3. Combine buttermilk, soda, eggs, cinnamon and vanilla. Stir into chocolate mixture.
4. Stir in flour, blending well. Pour into 9" x 13" pan that has been greased and floured. Bake for 30 minutes or until toothpick inserted in center comes out clean. Frost with Collins Chocolate Frosting (see Index).

Serves 12.

Las cuentas claras y el chocolate espeso.

Agreements should be clearly expressed and chocolate should be served thick.

Winter Oatmeal Cake

My good friend Barbara Gaines bakes this cake in the wintertime when company is coming. It's one of her favorites to serve - not only is it delicious, but her home is filled with its warm welcoming fragrances while the cake is baking.

1¼ cups boiling water
1 cup old fashioned oats
½ cup butter or margarine
2 eggs
1 cup sugar
1 cup brown sugar
1⅓ cups flour
½ teaspoon salt
1 teaspoon nutmeg
1 teaspoon cinnamon
1 teaspoon soda
1 teaspoon vanilla
Nuts, raisins and dates, optional

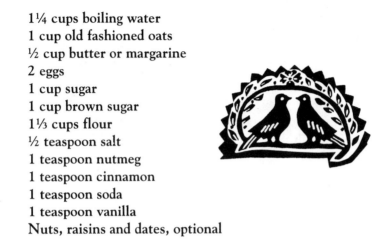

1. Preheat oven to 350 degrees.
2. Pour boiling water over oats and butter or margarine. Let stand for 20 minutes.
3. Mix eggs, sugar, brown sugar and add to oat mixture. Add remaining ingredients until thoroughly combined.
4. Bake for 30 to 35 minutes in 9" x 13" pan which has been spray coated. Add topping while cake is warm.

Topping:
½ cup evaporated milk
½ cup butter or margarine, softened
¾ cup brown sugar
1 cup coconut, shredded
¾ cup pecans, chopped

Combine all ingredients and pour over cake.

Serves 12.

Note: This cake is especially good served warm. Barbara likes to warm individual slices in the microwave when serving.

Old Fashioned Hot Milk Cake

David and Carlos like this cake on their birthdays. It's not a fancy cake - just plain GOOD! When they were little boys, I would wrap coins in wax paper and place them in the middle of the cake before frosting. They loved the surprise when they found quarters or half dollars.

1 cup milk
½ cup butter
4 eggs
2 cups sugar
2 cups flour
2 teaspoons baking powder
¼ teaspoon salt
1 teaspoon vanilla

1. Preheat oven to 350 degrees.

2. In a sauce pan or microwave, heat the milk and butter until the butter is melted and the milk scalded.

3. In mixing bowl, beat the eggs well. Gradually beat in the sugar. Stir in the flour, baking powder and salt.

4. Pour the milk mixture into the egg mixture and add the vanilla. Using a whisk, mix well.

5. Pour batter into a greased 9" x 13" cake pan. Bake the cake for 25 to 30 minutes.

6. Frost with Collins Chocolate Frosting or Citrus Nut Frosting (recipes following).

Serves 12.

Note: When making frosting, double or triple your recipe. Measure into containers and keep in your refrigerator until your next cake. It's really handy!

Citrus Nut Frosting

A light, creamy frosting, and bursting with zesty citrus flavor!

½ cup butter, softened
8 ounces cream cheese
1 pound powdered sugar
Zest of 1 lemon
1 tablespoon lemon juice
Zest of 1 orange
1 tablespoon orange juice
¼ teaspoon vanilla
½ cup walnuts, toasted and finely chopped

1. Using an electric mixer or food processor, cream butter and cream cheese. Add powdered sugar slowly, blending thoroughly.

2. Add the remaining ingredients and pulse just to mix. Be careful not to over process.

Makes frosting for one 9" x 13" sheet cake.

Collins Chocolate Frosting

This family recipe is in both of my books, and any future ones, because I've never found another I like better. A great frosting on any cake!

½ cup butter, softened
¾ cup cocoa
3 cups powdered sugar
1 teaspoon vanilla
¼ cup brewed coffee

1. Using an electric mixer or food processor, cream butter. Add cocoa, blending well.

2. Add powdered sugar and vanilla.

3. Add coffee, a little at a time, until spreading consistency. Add more coffee, a few drops at a time if the frosting is too thick.

Makes frosting for one 9" x 13" cake.

Apricot Savannah Cake

I like the combination of flavors in chocolate dipped apricots. This cake is similar and I love it!

1 cup dried apricots, chopped coarsely
½ cup dry sherry
¾ cup butter, room temperature
¼ cup brown sugar
¾ cup white sugar
3 eggs
1½ teaspoons vanilla
Zest of 1 orange
2½ cups flour
1½ teaspoons baking soda
½ teaspoon salt
1½ cups buttermilk
½ cup toasted walnuts, chopped
1 cup semi-sweet chocolate chips, chopped coarsely

1. Soak apricots in sherry for several hours or overnight.

2. Preheat oven to 350 degrees.

3. Using an electric mixer, cream the butter and the sugars together in a large bowl. Add the eggs, one at a time, beating well after each addition. Beat in the vanilla and the orange zest.

4. Combine the flour, baking soda, and salt. Add alternately with the buttermilk, beating well after each addition. Stir in the apricots with the sherry, walnuts and chocolate chips.

5. Pour the batter into 3 greased and floured 9" round cake pans. Bake for 35 to 40 minutes or until toothpick inserted in center comes out clean. Cool cakes in pans for 10 minutes. Invert on wire racks and cool completely. Spread the Chocolate Ganache between the layers while the cake is still warm. Use the Cream Cheese Frosting to frost the sides and top of the cake. Press the walnuts onto the lower half on side of cake.

Viele Hunde sind des Hasen Tod.

Chocolate Ganache:
    1½ cups semi-sweet chocolate chips
    1 cup heavy whipping cream

    1. Melt the chocolate slowly.

    2. Pour the melted chocolate into a mixing bowl. Using a whisk, pour the whipping cream slowly into the chocolate. Continue to mix until smooth.

    3. Spread the ganache between the cake layers while the cake and the ganache are still warm.

Cream Cheese Frosting:
    ¼ cup butter, room temperature
    8 oz. cream cheese, room temperature
    1 pound powdered sugar
    2 tablespoons orange liqueur
    2 tablespoons orange zest

Using an electric mixer, cream the butter and cream cheese. Add the powdered sugar and orange liqueur. Beat until smooth and add the zest. This frosts three layers and sides of cake.

Serves 12 to 14.

Many dogs are the hare's death.

Pumpkin Pecan Cake

In the fall during hunting season, I enjoy serving this cake. Men especially like it. It's also nice to have during the holidays when family comes to visit.

3½ cups flour
2 teaspoons baking soda
2 teaspoons baking powder
1 teaspoon salt
2 teaspoons cinnamon
½ teaspoon ginger
½ teaspoon allspice
½ teaspoon nutmeg
½ teaspoon cloves
1 cup unsalted butter, room temperature
1¼ cups sugar
½ cup dark brown sugar, firmly packed
4 large eggs, room temperature
1⅔ cups canned solid pack pumpkin
½ cup sour cream
¼ cup molasses
2 tablespoons dark rum
1½ cups pecans, toasted and chopped
½ cup crystallized ginger, minced

1. Position rack in lowest third of oven and preheat to 350 degrees.
2. Mix flour, baking soda, baking powder, salt and spices in medium bowl. Set aside.
3. Using electric mixer, cream butter with both sugars in large bowl until very light and fluffy. Add eggs 1 at a time, beating well after each addition. Beat in pumpkin, sour cream, molasses and rum. Mix in dry ingredients, pecans and ginger.
4. Pour batter into greased and floured bundt pan. Bake until tester inserted near center of cake comes out clean, about 1 hour and 15 minutes. Cool cake 15 minutes in pan on rack. Turn cake out onto rack, glaze and let cool.

Buttermilk Glaze:
- ½ cup sugar
- ¼ cup buttermilk
- ¼ cup butter
- 1 tablespoon corn syrup
- ½ teaspoon baking soda
- 1 teaspoon vanilla

1. In a sauce pan, measure in the sugar, buttermilk, butter, corn syrup and baking soda. Boil 5 to 6 minutes until thick and syrupy.

2. Add vanilla and pour over the cake.

Serves 16.

Black Forest Cake

A beautiful cake to enjoy anytime you want to serve a dessert that is light tasting and not too filling.

6 eggs, separated
1¼ cups sugar
¾ cup flour, sifted
¼ cup unsweetened cocoa
¼ teaspoon salt
1 teaspoon vanilla
1 tablespoon water
¼ cup sugar
¼ cup brandy
1 can dark sweet canned cherries, drained
Garnish: Shaved chocolate and remaining cherries

1. Have all ingredients at room temperature.

2. Preheat oven to 350 degrees.

3. Using an electric mixer, beat egg whites until soft peaks form. Slowly add ½ cup sugar and beat until consistency of meringue.

4. Sift flour once. Add cocoa and salt and sift again.

5. Beat egg yolks, add ¾ cup sugar and vanilla. Add flour mixture and egg white mixture alternately to the egg yolks, folding carefully.

6. Pour batter into 3 floured and greased 9" cake pans. Bake for approximately 25 minutes. Remove from oven.

7. Mix together the water, sugar and brandy. Stir until dissolved. Brush on warm cake layers.

8. Frost 3 layers and sides of cooled cake with frosting. Place ⅓ cup cherries between layers. Garnish with shaved chocolate and remaining cherries. Refrigerate for 3 hours before serving. Can be made and assembled the day before serving.

Frosting:
    2 cups whipping cream
    ¼ cup powdered sugar
    2 tablespoons brandy

1. Using an electric mixer, beat the cream and sugar until soft peaks form. Add the brandy. Makes enough for a 3-layer cake.

Serves 12.

Rum Raisin Cheesecake

A delicious finale for an Italian dinner.

Crust:
  1 cup old fashioned or quick oats
  ¼ cup nuts, chopped
  3 tablespoons brown sugar, packed
  3 tablespoons margarine or butter, melted

1. Preheat oven to 350 degrees.
2. Mix the crust ingredients and press into the bottom of a well-buttered 9" to 10" springform pan. Bake 15 minutes. Remove from oven.

Filling:
  4 8-ounce packages cream cheese, softened
  ⅔ cup sugar
  ½ cup flour
  4 eggs
  1 cup sour cream
  6 tablespoons rum
  4 tablespoons margarine or butter
  ⅔ cup brown sugar, packed
  ⅔ cup raisins
  ½ cup nuts, chopped
  4 tablespoons old fashioned or quick oats

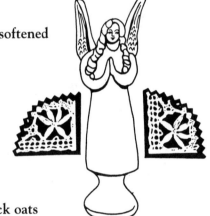

1. Using an electric mixer, beat the softened cream cheese with the sugar and 2 tablespoons flour until well blended.
2. Add the eggs one at a time, blending well after each. Blend in sour cream and rum. Pour into prepared pan.
3. In a medium mixing bowl, cut margarine or butter into the remaining flour and brown sugar until mixture resembles coarse crumbs. Stir in raisins, nuts and oats. Sprinkle evenly over cream cheese mixture.
4. Pour batter into baked crust.
5. Bake 1 hour at 350 degrees. Turn oven off and let the cheesecake cool in oven with the door closed for several hours or overnight. Refrigerate.

Serves 14 to 16.

Toffee Cheesecake with Caramel Topping

Mmmm good. Toffee and cheesecake! What a great combination.

Crust:

>   1½ cups graham cracker crumbs
>   6 tablespoons unsalted butter, melted
>   ¼ cup dark brown sugar, firmly packed

Mix the crust ingredients together thoroughly and press into the bottom of a well-buttered 9" to 10" springform pan. The crust should rise one inch up the sides of the pan. Refrigerate crust.

Filling:

>   2 pounds cream cheese, room temperature
>   1½ cups sugar
>   5 large eggs, room temperature
>   2½ teaspoons vanilla extract
>   2 teaspoons fresh lemon juice

1. Preheat oven to 350 degrees.
2. Using mixer, beat cream cheese until fluffy. Add sugar and beat until smooth. Beat in eggs one at a time. Mix in vanilla and fresh lemon juice.
3. Pour filling into the prepared crust. Bake about one hour and 15 minutes, until cake rises about ½" over rim and the center moves slightly when pan is shaken.
4. Cool the cheesecake on a rack. The cake will fall as it cools, sinking in center. Cover and refrigerate until well chilled, at least 6 hours.

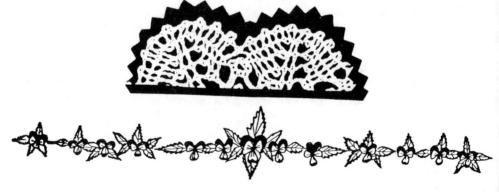

Caramel Topping:
- ¼ cup butter
- 1 cup brown sugar
- ¼ cup milk
- 1 teaspoon vanilla
- Dash salt
- 2 tablespoons walnuts, toasted and chopped

1. Heat butter and sugar in heavy saucepan over low heat, stirring until sugar dissolves and butter melts. Add milk and vanilla and salt. Boil for 3 minutes.

2. Using small sharp knife, cut around sides of pan to loosen cake. Release pan sides. Pour sauce into center of cake and spread evenly. Sprinkle with walnuts. Chill cake until caramel topping is set. Refrigerate until served.

Serves 14 to 16.

White Chocolate Brownie Cheesecake

We serve this in our Tea Room on a pool of raspberry sauce* and chocolate fudge drizzled on top. It's a new favorite of our customers!

Crust:

1½ cups graham cracker crumbs
¼ cup ground pecans
½ cup unsweetened cocoa
¼ cup plus 1 tablespoon butter, melted
¼ cup sugar

1. Preheat oven to 350 degrees.
2. Mix the crust ingredients thoroughly and press into the bottom of a well-buttered 9" to 10" springform pan. Bake 15 minutes. Remove from oven.

Filling:

1 pound white chocolate, chopped
4 8-ounce packages cream cheese, softened
½ cup sour cream
¼ cup sugar
1 teaspoon vanilla extract
1 teaspoon almond extract
4 eggs
2 cups Peach Tree Chocolate Brownies, chopped into small chunks (see Index).

1. Reduce heat to 300 degrees.
2. Melt white chocolate in a sauce pan and set aside.

La gloria y el infierno están aquí en la tierra.

3. Using an electric mixer, beat softened cream cheese with sour cream and sugar until well blended.

4. Add the vanilla extract, almond extract, and the eggs, one at a time, blending well after each.

5. Pour half of the filling into the prepared pan. Layer the brownies evenly over the filling. Pour the remaining filling over the brownies.

6. Bake 1 hour at 300 degrees. Turn off oven and let cool in oven with the door closed for several hours or overnight. Refrigerate.

Serves 14 to 16.

Note: Strain heated raspberry jam through a sieve.

Heaven and Hell are here on earth.

Notes

_____

_____

_____

_____

_____

_____

_____

_____

_____

_____

_____

_____

_____

Desserts

Electra Sorbet with Fresh Crushed Peaches

This is probably one of the most amazing peach desserts I've ever tasted. It is soooo creamy and has not a hint of fat!

1½ cups sugar
½ cup water
½ cup Electra California Orange Muscat Wine
2 cups peaches, fresh or frozen, crushed
Juice of 1½ to 2 lemons, unstrained
2 egg whites
2 tablespoons Electra California Orange Muscat Wine
Garnish: Mint leaves

1. Mix together sugar, water and Electra wine and stir mixture over very low heat until sugar is dissolved. Boil the mixture steadily for 5 minutes.

2. Remove from heat and add peaches and lemon juice.

3. Cool mixture thoroughly and stir in stiffly beaten egg whites and 2 tablespoons of Electra wine.

4. Freeze mixture in ice cream freezer. You can serve immediately or store in freezer. Garnish with fresh mint leaves.

Makes 6 cups.

Note: If you can't find Electra California Muscat Wine, Peach Brandy is a good substitute.

Dem stillen Veilchen gleich, Das im verborgenen bleuht ist immer fromm und gut Auch wenn es niemand sieht.

Beal Family Favorite Ice Cream

Helana's mom began a mouth-watering tradition of making homemade ice cream for family and guests every summer weekend they spent at their lake house. Now, the humming of an ice cream maker quickly reminds Helana of those sunny days with her family.

9 to 10 eggs, separated
2 cups sugar
1 14-ounce can Eagle Brand Condensed Milk
1 12-ounce can evaporated milk
1 4-ounce box Junket vanilla ice cream mix (not tablets)
1 pint whipping cream
1 quart half and half
1 tablespoon vanilla
Milk

1. Beat egg whites until soft peaks form. Beat in egg yolks and sugar.
2. Mix in condensed milk and evaporated milk and pour mixture into ice cream freezer can (6-quart size).
3. Combine Junket, whipping cream, half and half and vanilla. Beat about 2 minutes and pour mixture into ice cream freezer can. If necessary, add milk to fill line.
4. Start ice cream motor without salt or ice in bucket. Let run for 2 minutes to thoroughly mix ingredients.
5. Add ice and salt to freezer. Should be ready in 25 to 30 minutes.

Note: If not served immediately, the ice cream is best if it's stored in a plastic container in freezer.

Be like the little violet that blooms unseen.
Always kind and good even if nobody sees you.

Crème Brulée

This is probably my very favorite dessert - the ingredients are so simple and basic. It's especially good served after Italian or Mexican food, and the servings can be small - just a nice way to end the meal!

8 egg yolks
5 tablespoons white sugar
2 tablespoons vanilla extract
2 pints light cream, scalded
½ cup brown sugar* or natural sugar

1. Preheat oven to 325 degrees. In a large bowl, beat the egg yolks until lemon color.

2. Blend in white sugar and vanilla.

3. Combine cream and egg mixture.

4. Pour into a shallow 10" baking dish. Set the dish in a pan of water filled half way to rim of baking dish.

5. Bake for 1 hour and 20 minutes. When firm, remove from oven. When cooled, refrigerate it. When chilled thoroughly, and just before you are ready to serve, sprinkle brown sugar* evenly on top to a depth of ⅛ ".

6. Place directly under broiler so sugar caramelizes - one or two minutes. Be careful not to let sugar burn. Serve immediately after caramelizing the sugar. If you wait longer than 30 minutes, the sugar will become weepy.

*Note: It is sometimes difficult to sprinkle the brown sugar on the Brulée evenly. I've solved this problem by placing the brown sugar in a shallow pan in the oven at 325 degrees for 10 to 15 minutes, until it becomes dry. Then place sugar in the bowl of a food processor until the sugar is smooth and not lumpy. Now it is much easier to achieve a smooth surface.

Serves 8 to 10.

Bluh wie das Veilchen im Moose bescheiden, sittsam und rein, und nicht wie die stolze Rose, die nur bewundert will sein.

Tiramisu

I'm often surprised when I order Tiramisu in restaurants because everyone seems to have their own version. This is similar to the way I had it at a restaurant in Washington, D.C. - the first time I had ever tried it - and the very best!

4 eggs, separated
¼ cup Kahlua liqueur
1 pound marscapone cheese
½ cup sugar
1 7-ounce package Lady Fingers
½ cup espresso coffee
⅓ cup chocolate morsels, finely grated

1. Mix together egg yolks, Kahlua, marscapone cheese and sugar and set aside.
2. Beat egg whites until frothy soft peaks form. Fold two mixtures together.
3. Dip each Lady Finger quickly in espresso*.
4. Layer Lady Fingers in 9" x 13" dish. Pour half marscapone mixture over Lady Finger layer. Add another layer Lady Fingers and remaining marscapone mixture.
5. Sprinkle top with grated chocolate.
6. Chill overnight.

Serves 10 to 12.

*Note: When dipping the lady fingers into the espresso, you must work quickly, so they don't disintegrate.

Flourish like the violet modest, virtuous and pure. Don't be like the arrogant rose which only asks for admiration.

Cream Puffs

When Evelyn makes these for our Tea Room "dessert of the day", everyone reserves their's pronto.

½ cup butter or margarine
1 cup boiling water
1 cup sifted all purpose flour
4 eggs

1. Preheat oven to 400 degrees.

2. Put butter or margarine and boiling water in a sauce pan. Heat until thoroughly melted. Add flour, all at once, and stir vigorously. Cook until mixture is thick and smooth and does not stick to side of pan; stir constantly so it will not burn. Place mixture in a mixing bowl and thoroughly beat in one egg at a time.

3. Drop by rounded tablespoon on a greased baking sheet - 1½" apart. Bake for 35 minutes. When cool, make a small opening and fill with favorite filling, sweetened cream or ice cream.

Serves 8.

Vanilla Filling:
4 cups milk
6 tablespoons sugar
4 tablespoons flour
Dash of salt
3 eggs, beaten
1 tablespoon vanilla

1. Scald 3½ cups milk with 4 tablespoons of sugar. Mix well flour, salt and remaining 2 tablespoons sugar. Stir in remaining ½ cup milk. Add eggs and mix thoroughly.

2. Combine with scalded milk mixture (adding a small amount at a time to prevent cooking eggs). Cook until thick, stirring constantly. Cool; add vanilla and chill.

Lemon Filling:

½ stick butter
1 cup sugar
4 tablespoons flour
2 cups milk
2 eggs, beaten
Zest of 1 lemon and juice

1. Melt butter; add sugar and flour, blending well. Gradually add milk. Heat in double boiler until it begins to thicken.
2. Mix eggs, lemon juice, and zest.
3. Gradually add about 1 cup of the hot milk mixture to eggs. Combine the two mixtures and cook in top of double boiler until thick, stirring constantly.

Chocolate Filling:

1 cup sugar
¼ cup flour
2 squares chocolate, unsweetened
3 tablespoons butter
1¼ cups milk
1 egg, beaten
1 teaspoon vanilla extract

In a double boiler mix sugar and flour. Add chocolate and butter. Combine milk and egg and add to mixture. Cook over boiling water, stirring constantly. When mixture thickens, remove from heat, add vanilla and stir well.

Butterscotch Cream Filling:

1 cup brown sugar, packed
2 tablespoons cornstarch
1 dash salt
2 eggs, beaten
2 cups milk
1 teaspoon vanilla
2 tablespoons butter

1. Combine the brown sugar, cornstarch and salt.
2. Combine eggs, milk and brown sugar mixture. Whisk everything together well and microwave for 5 minutes.
3. Whisk the pudding again and return to microwave for another 5 minutes. Whisk again and add vanilla and butter.

Oma Stehling's Sweet Rice

Oma and Opa Stehling took care of our three children when they were little and our Peach Tree business was just beginning. Sweet Rice was one of the treats Oma served at her homey kitchen table. Tina was able to get this recipe from Oma's daughter, Irene Keller, and keep the memories going!

1 cup long grain white rice
6 cups milk
¾ to 1 cup sugar
Cinnamon

1. In a medium saucepan, cook the rice in the milk for about 1½ hours on low heat. Stir frequently to keep the rice from burning.
2. When the rice has absorbed most of the milk, add the sugar, stir well, turn off the heat. Add sugar according to taste.
3. Let the rice set and the rest of the milk will be absorbed. Sprinkle with cinnamon.

Serves 8 to 10.

Apple Bread Pudding

Serve this scrumptious dessert warm in a pool of creamy Custard Sauce (recipe following). It's pure comfort food at it's best!

6 cups dry French bread, cubed
4 cups sliced apples
4 tablespoons butter
¼ cup sugar
⅓ cup raisins, or dried apricots, soaked in 2 tablespoons brandy

Custard:
5 eggs
4 cups milk
⅔ cup brown sugar
1 teaspoon vanilla
2 tablespoons butter
1 tablespoon sugar

1. Preheat oven to 350 degrees.

2. Measure custard ingredients into a blender or whisk them together.

3. Soak bread in custard. Set aside while you continue with apple mixture.

4. Sauté apples in butter for 5 minutes. Mix in sugar and caramelize over medium-high heat for 3 to 5 minutes. Watch carefully! Add raisins or apricots and brandy. Cook together for 1 or 2 minutes.

5. Spread the apple mixture in an 8-cup baking dish (wider than it is deep). Pour bread-custard mixture over fruit.

6. Dust the pudding with sugar and dot with butter. Bake for 1 hour. Serve warm with Custard Sauce (recipe following).

Serves 10.

Custard Sauce

You'll find many uses for this Custard Sauce - easy to make, and so handy. It makes a delicious dress up for leftover cakes, and is nice poured over fresh fruit for a light finish to a hearty meal.

2 cups half and half
4 egg yolks
¼ cup sugar
1 teaspoon vanilla

1. Heat cream to scalding in heavy saucepan.

2. Using a whisk, beat egg yolks with sugar. Pour small amount of hot milk into egg mixture, stirring well. Gradually add egg mixture to remaining hot milk.

3. Cook mixture over medium heat, stirring constantly, until custard coats metal spoon. Remove from heat and add vanilla.* Serve warm or cold.

Makes 2 cups.

*Note: If the custard should curdle while cooking, place mixture in blender, and blend until very smooth, about 30 seconds.

Blackberry Cobbler

In Fredericksburg, blackberries appear in fruit stands in early May, just before peach season. We're always glad to get this seasonal fruit and bake a cobbler for our customers because it's always a hit! When we serve it, it's usually ordered with a scoop of vanilla ice cream on top.

Fruit Mixture:
- 8 cups blackberries
- ¾ cup sugar
- 6 tablespoons tapioca
- ¼ teaspoon cinnamon
- 2 tablespoons lemon juice

Cobbler Dough:
- 8 tablespoons butter, softened
- ¾ cup sugar
- 2 cups flour
- 1½ cups milk
- 2 teaspoons baking powder
- 1 teaspoon salt

Cobbler Topping:
- 1 cup sugar
- 2 tablespoons cornstarch
- 1¼ cups boiling water
- Cinnamon

1. Preheat oven to 375 degrees.
2. In a mixing bowl, combine all ingredients to make **Fruit Mixture**. Mix thoroughly. Pour the **Fruit Mixture** into a buttered 9" x 13" baking dish.
3. In a bowl mix thoroughly all ingredients for **Cobbler Dough**. Spread over **Fruit Mixture**.
4. In a medium mixing bowl, stir together dry **Cobbler Topping** ingredients. Sprinkle evenly over the **Cobbler Dough** layer. Pour boiling water evenly over the cobbler. Sprinkle with cinnamon.
5. Bake for 1 hour until the top has a golden crust.

Serves 15.

Old Fashioned Peach Cobbler

This is the very popular peach cobbler that Peggy Cox introduced to our customers when she was Tea Room manager. It's an incredible crowd pleaser -- Enjoy!!

Fruit Mixture:
    6 tablespoons tapioca
    6 or 7 cups fresh Fredericksburg peaches, sliced
    1 cup sugar
    ¼ teaspoon cinnamon
    ¼ teaspoon nutmeg

Cobbler Dough:
    ½ cup butter, softened
    1 cup sugar
    2 cups flour
    1½ cups milk
    2 teaspoons baking powder
    1 teaspoon salt

Cobbler Topping:
    1½ cups sugar
    2 tablespoons cornstarch
    Cinnamon
    Nutmeg
    ½ cup boiling water

1. Preheat oven to 375 degrees.

2. In a mixing bowl, combine all ingredients to make **Fruit Mixture**. Mix thoroughly. Pour the Fruit Mixture into a buttered 9" x 13" baking dish.

3. In a bowl mix thoroughly all ingredients for **Cobbler Dough**. Spread over **Fruit Mixture**.

4. In a medium mixing bowl, stir together dry **Cobbler Topping** ingredients. Sprinkle evenly over the **Cobbler Dough** layer. Pour boiling water evenly over the cobbler.

5. Bake for 1 hour and 20 minutes or until knife inserted comes out clean and the top has a golden crust.

Serves 15.

 Christmas Trifle

*Our Peach Tree Christmas party **always** includes trifle for dessert. The tradition began when our business was small and we celebrated together with a progressive dinner.*

The grand finale to the evening was spent at my mother's house with candlelight, gift exchange around her tree, and her homemade trifle, served from clear crystal bowls so we could see the pretty layers. We've changed the tradition a little now because our Peach Tree family is much larger - but the trifle still reigns for dessert!!

1 cup raspberry jam, strained through coarse sieve or 1 cup strawberry jam, unstrained
1 pound cake, sliced, ½" thick (1 pound)
6 tablespoons sherry
2 cups fruit*
1 recipe Custard Sauce (see Index)
2 cups whipped cream
Garnish: Fresh fruit

1. In an 8-cup dish, begin assembling with a small amount of raspberry jam or strawberry jam (for color). Layer slices of pound cake. Sprinkle 2 tablespoons of sherry over cake. Next, a thin layer of jam, followed by fruit layer. Spoon on custard layer.

2. Depending on the shape of your dish, you can do one or two more layers as directed.

3. Refrigerate overnight. Top with whipped cream just before serving. Garnish with fresh fruit.

Serves 8 to 10.

*Note: Fresh or frozen cherries, blueberries, raspberries, strawberries, or blackberries can be used - or a combination of your choosing.

Note: A dear lady from England once told me that to make a "proper trifle" you simply toss in a "trifle of this and a trifle of that"! Be creative, and begin your own trifle tradition.

Pies

Cynthia's Basic Pie and Pastry Crust

This is the pastry crust that we use daily in the Tea Room to make our quiches. If you are careful to use chilled ingredients and work the dough lightly, your results will be a tender flaky crust - for desserts, meat pies and quiches! Bon Appétit!

1½ cups unsifted unbleached flour
½ teaspoon salt
2 tablespoons Crisco shortening
6 tablespoons CHILLED butter (not margarine)
5 tablespoons ICED water

1. Mix flour and salt in bowl. Cut in Crisco and butter with a pastry blender until crumble.
2. Add **ICED** water, a little at a time, mixing with a fork until well blended. Place dough into plastic bag and gently press dough together into flat disk. Refrigerate dough for 30 to 60 minutes. This allows the gluten to develop in the dough.
3. Carefully roll dough on floured board; lift into 9" to 10" pie plate, trimming dough and rolling edges under to form rim. Flute the edge. It is important not to overwork your pastry at this point; if you handle it gently, your result will be a flaky and tender crust.
4. Put a layer of foil over dough, and fill to the top with either pie weights or dry pinto beans. This prevents crust from puffing up and shrinking.

For PARTIALLY baked pie crust: Bake in a preheated 400 degree oven for 12 minutes. Carefully remove foil and beans. Prick crust bottom with fork several times, and bake 5 to 10 minutes more until completely dry.
For COMPLETELY baked pie crust: Bake in a preheated 400 degree oven for 12 minutes. Carefully remove foil and beans. Prick crust bottom with fork several times, and bake 10 to 15 minutes more until completely dry and golden in color.

Ich bin klein. Mein Herz ist rein. Soll neimand drin wohnen als Gott allein.

Brooke's Pie Crust

This is the pie crust that appears in our first cookbook. I'm repeating it for use with the pies we feature here because it's still among the very best!

3 cups sifted flour
1 teaspoon salt
1 cup Crisco shortening
1 beaten egg, plus enough iced water to make ½ cup

1. Mix flour and salt. Cut in shortening with a pastry blender until consistency of coarse corn meal.

2. Add egg and water mixture and mix well with a fork. Form into a ball.

3. Divide dough in half. On lightly floured surface, roll dough and gently lift into two 9" pie plates. Turn under edge and flute. The shells are now ready for filling.

Prebaked Crust for Cream Pies

1. Preheat oven to 400 degrees.

2. Put a layer of foil over dough and fill to top with either pie weights or dry pinto beans. This prevents crust from puffing up and shrinking.

3. Bake crust for 10 minutes.

4. Remove foil and prick crust bottom with fork several times, and bake 8 to 10 minutes longer, until golden. The crust is ready to fill.

Makes 2 shells.

I am small. My heart is pure. May only the spirit of God dwell there in.

Grandma's Chocolate Pie

On Mother's Day, I would bake one each of the Chocolate and Caramel pies for my mother because she loved them so much. It reminded here of her Grandmother Roessler and times spent with her.

1½ cups sugar
3 egg yolks
¼ cup flour
2 cups milk
6 tablespoons cocoa
2 tablespoons butter
½ teaspoon vanilla
1 Cynthia's Basic Pie and Pastry Crust, baked and cooled (see Index)
1 recipe Perfect Meringue (see Index)

1. Combine all ingredients in sauce pan, except butter and vanilla. Cook over medium heat until thickened.
2. Add butter and vanilla. Pour into 9" cooled and baked pastry shell.
3. Top with meringue and bake as per instructions (see Index).

Serves 8.

Fudge Walnut Pie, Texas Salad Nicoise,
Tuscan Bread, and Peach Margaritas

Grandma's Caramel Pie

1½ cups brown sugar
5 tablespoons flour
1½ cups milk
3 egg yolks
3 tablespoons butter
1 teaspoon vanilla
1 Cynthia's Basic Pie and Pastry Crust, baked and cooled (see Index)
1 recipe Perfect Meringue (see Index)

1. Combine all ingredients in sauce pan, except butter and vanilla. Cook over medium heat until thickened.
2. Add butter and vanilla. Pour into 9" cooled and baked pastry shell.
3. Top with meringue and bake as per instructions (see Index).

Serves 8.

Banana Caramel Pie

When we have our Peach Tree Employee picnics in the summertime, Tom Richard's wife, Verna, brings's this pie and it's always a race to see who can get some before it's all gone. It's scrumptious!

1 can Eagle Brand Condensed milk
1 Brooke's Pie Crust, baked and cooled (see Index)
4 medium bananas - this may vary
½ pint whipping cream, whipped and lightly sweetened
3 small Heath candy bars - frozen, chopped

1. Place unopened can of condensed milk in sauce pan (remove the label). Cover the can with water and simmer 4 to 5 hours. Add more water as needed. Remove and let can cool.
2. Line the pie shell with sliced bananas. (I like a lot of bananas because the caramel is very sweet.) Pour caramelized milk over the bananas. Spread the whipped cream on top.
3. Sprinkle chopped Heath Bars over the whipped cream.

Serves 8.

Gammy's Lemon Pie

When I make this pie, I like to fold 1 to 2 teaspoons of lemon zest into the meringue - it's a nice touch!

2 tablespoon butter
1½ cups sugar
3 tablespoons corn starch
2 cups water
3 egg yolks, beaten
Zest of 1 lemon
Juice of 1½ lemons
1 Cynthia's Basic Pie and Pastry Crust, baked and cooled (see Index)
1 recipe Perfect Meringue (recipe on opposite page)

1. Melt butter, add sugar and corn starch, blending well. Gradually add water. Heat in sauce pan over medium heat until it begins to thicken.
2. Combine egg yolks, lemon zest and juice.
3. Gradually add about 1 cup of hot mixture to eggs. Combine the two mixtures and cook until thickened, stirring constantly.
4. Pour into baked and cooled 9" pastry crust.
5. Top with meringue and follow baking instructions.

Coconut Cream Pie

This is the kind of pie you find in hidden away small town cafes - showcased under glass - and irresistible!!

2 cups milk
⅓ cup flour
¼ teaspoon salt
3 eggs
¾ cup sugar
1 teaspoon vanilla
2 tablespoons butter
1⅓ cups grated coconut
1 Cynthia's Basic Pie and Pastry Crust, baked and cooled (see Index)
1 recipe Perfect Meringue (recipe on opposite page)
2 tablespoons coconut

1. Scald 1½ cups milk. Stir flour and salt into remaining ½ cup milk. Add mixture to hot milk. Cook, stirring frequently for 20 minutes.

2. Beat eggs with sugar. Slowly pour into hot mixture. Cook for two minutes.

3. Add vanilla, butter and coconut, after removing from stove. Cool.

4. Pour into baked and cooled 9" pastry crust.

5. Top with meringue, sprinkle with coconut, and follow baking instructions.

Serves 8.

Perfect Meringue

3 egg whites, room temperature
½ teaspoon vanilla
¼ teaspoon cream of tartar
6 tablespoons sugar

1. Preheat oven to 375 degrees.

2. Beat egg whites with vanilla and cream of tartar until soft peaks form. (Whites will whip fluffier if they are at room temperature.) Gradually add sugar, beating until stiff and glossy and all sugar is dissolved.

3. Spread meringue over pie filling (at room temperature), sealing meringue to edges of pastry all around. This prevents shrinking.

4. Bake for 12 to 15 minutes or until meringue is golden. Cool thoroughly before serving.

Makes meringue for 1 pie.

Note: Beat meringue until very stiff, be careful though, that it isn't too dry. Underbeating the meringue will cause it to weep (edges will liquefy). Overbeating will produce a lumpy meringue. In cooking class I was told the correct way to know if it's right is to hold the bowl over my head - upside down. If it stays in the bowl the meringue is good!

Fudge Walnut Pie

Super rich and super good! A special treat for chocolate lovers - with a tall glass of ice cold milk!

½ cup butter (not margarine)
1 cup sugar
½ teaspoon salt
1 teaspoon vanilla
1 cup light corn syrup
3 eggs, beaten
2 teaspoons fresh lemon juice
1 cup walnuts, chopped and toasted
1 cup semi-sweet chocolate chips
1 Brooke's Pie Crust, unbaked (see Index)

1.Preheat oven to 425 degrees.
2.In saucepan, brown butter until golden. Watch carefully not to burn. Cool.
3.Add sugar, salt, vanilla, syrup and beaten eggs, mixing well. Add lemon juice, walnuts and chocolate chips.
4.Pour into unbaked pie shell, and bake for 10 minutes. Reduce to 325 degrees and bake for additional 55 minutes, or until center is firm. Cool on rack.

Serves 8.

Des menschen Gluck auf Erden ist lieben
und geliebt zu werden.

Old Fashioned Deep Dish Apple Pie

Apple pie is pure comfort food and this is a great recipe to use when you are short on time. It goes together quickly - doesn't require a lot of fuss.

1 recipe Cynthia's Basic Pie and Pastry Crust (see Index)
8 to 9 Granny Smith apples, peeled and thinly sliced
½ teaspoon cinnamon
½ cup sugar
Juice of 1 lemon
Zest of 1 lemon

1. Preheat oven to 400 degrees.
2. Follow Cynthia's Basic Pie and Pastry Crust recipe, with a slight variation in placing of the crust. Use a 10" deep dish pie plate. Lay the pastry in pie plate letting the edges drape over the side of the plate.
3. Combine all ingredients in a large bowl and toss thoroughly to coat the apples.
4. Pour the apples into the unbaked crust. Then bring pastry edges randomly over apples. Sprinkle the topping over the apples and bake the pie for 15 minutes.
5. Reduce heat to 350 degrees and bake for 45 to 50 minutes.

Topping:
    ⅓ cup butter
    3 tablespoons brown sugar, packed
    3 tablespoons white sugar
    ½ teaspoon cinnamon
    ½ cup walnuts, toasted and chopped
    ½ cup oats
    ½ teaspoon nutmeg

Combine all ingredients thoroughly.

Serves 8 to 10.

It is the good fortune of man on earth to love and be loved in return.

Whole Wheat Turnovers

These are simple to make and ideal to pack for a picnic. They can be varied by using strawberry, blueberry or apricot preserves instead of apricot.

Pastry:
    ¾ cup whole wheat flour
    ¾ cup unbleached flour
    1 tablespoon brown sugar
    ¼ teaspoon salt
    ½ cup butter or margarine
    ½ cup sour cream

1. Stir together flours, sugar and salt. Cut in butter until mixture resembles coarse crumbs. Add sour cream and mix well, until mixture forms a ball. Refrigerate dough for 30 minutes or overnight.

2. Divide into 10 portions. On a lightly floured surface, roll each portion into a 4½" circle.

Filling:
    ½ cup peach preserves
    ½ cup coconut, flaked
    ½ cup golden raisins
    ½ cup pecans, roasted and chopped

1. Preheat oven to 375 degrees.

2. Combine preserves, coconut, raisins and pecans. Place 2 table-spoons filling atop each circle. Fold one side of dough over filling. Seal edges by pressing with tines of fork.

3. Place on ungreased baking sheet. Bake for 25 minutes or until lightly browned. Cool slightly on wire rack.

Powdered Sugar Glaze:
    ½ cup sifted powdered sugar
    ¼ teaspoon vanilla
    1 tablespoon milk

Drizzle with mixture of powdered sugar, vanilla and enough milk to make a "drizzle" consistency.

Serves 10.

Empanadas

Empanadas are the traditional pies of Mexico. They are usually fried - but I enjoy the baked ones just as much.

Filling:
- 2 cups sweet potatoes, mashed
- ⅓ cup brown sugar
- 1 teaspoon cinnamon
- ½ teaspoon anise seed, ground
- ¼ teaspoon allspice

Mix all ingredients and set aside.

Pastry:
- 2 cups unbleached flour
- 1 teaspoon salt
- 2 teaspoons baking powder
- ½ cup Crisco
- ⅓ cup ice water
- 2 tablespoons sugar
- 1 tablespoon cinnamon

1. Preheat oven to 425 degrees.

2. Mix flour, salt and baking powder. Cut in shortening with a pastry blender until consistency of coarse corn meal. Add ice water and mix well with a fork.

3. Divide dough and form into 12 balls. Let rest for 10 minutes in refrigerator.

4. Roll out into 4½" circle and fill with 2 tablespoons of filling. Fold one side of dough over filling. Seal edges by pressing with times of fork. Sprinkle with sugar and cinnamon mixture.

5. Place on ungreased cookie sheet and bake for 15 minutes or until golden brown.

Serves 12.

Peanut Butter and Jam Tarts

Delicious with a glass of ice cold milk - for kids of any age!!

1½ cups flour
2 teaspoons sugar
Pinch of salt
6 tablespoons cold butter
4 tablespoons Crisco
6 tablespoons ice water
1¼ cups peanut butter
1¼ cups jam

1. Preheat oven to 350 degrees.
2. Mix flour, sugar and salt. Cut in butter and Crisco with a pastry blender until consistency of coarse corn meal.
3. Add water and mix lightly with a fork. Form into a ball.
4. Divide dough into 15 balls. Roll out into 4" circles.
5. Place 1 tablespoon each of peanut butter and jam in the center of the circle. Fold in half, seal and crimp the edges.
6. Bake for 30 to 40 minutes until golden. Remove to rack to cool.

Glaze:
½ cup powdered sugar
1 tablespoon milk

Mix until smooth and spread on each tart.

Makes 15 tarts!

Sauces & Spreads

Arugula Pesto

One of my favorite taste discoveries this past year has been Arugula. I'm determined to use it as much as possible! This pesto is a must-do recipe. It's an exciting dress-up for pasta or it can be served as an appetizer, spread over Brie or goat cheese. Spread the pesto between layers of creamy goat cheese, ending up with pesto on top - sprinkle with a few extra pine nuts and serve with Tuscan Bread (see Index) or crackers. The bright green color of the pesto is a delight to the eye!

> 2 cups loosely packed arugula*
> ¼ cup olive oil
> 2 garlic cloves
> 2 tablespoons pine nuts, lightly toasted
> Salt to taste
> ¼ cup Parmesan cheese

1. Measure all ingredients, except the Parmesan cheese into food processor. Process until ingredients are thoroughly chopped.
2. Stir in cheese.
3. Refrigerate or freeze.

Makes ½ cup.

*Note: Arugula is a member of the mustard family, formerly known as roquette. It has a pungent peppery flavor. You'll find it in specialty food stores. I have friends who are growing it successfully from seeds. At the end of its season it puts on very unique looking white flowers - fun for garnishing!

Que no te hagan   de chivo los tamales

Summer Basil Pesto

Once you begin to make pesto, there are endless possibilities for creating. It's a meal when stirred into hot steaming pasta or over steamed veggies.

For a surprise appetizer, serve drizzled over cream cheese or goat cheese. Also, try a spoonful as a garnish when you serve minestrone. Tina and I like to make quantities in the summer when basil leaves are abundant and keep small batches in the freezer--ready for quick improvising.

4 garlic cloves
1 teaspoon salt
½ cup olive oil
2 cups fresh basil
¾ cup walnuts, or pine nuts, lightly toasted
1 teaspoon pepper, freshly ground
¾ cup Parmesan cheese, grated

Measure all ingredients, except for the Parmesan cheese, into food processor. Blend well. Stir in the cheese.

Makes 1½ cups.

Italian Olive Spread

This spread is great on our Tuscan Bread (see Index) layered with Italian meats, such as Capricola, salami and prosciutto. Make sandwiches and wrap in waxed paper and refrigerate until ready to serve. It's best if the sandwiches are made 4 to 6 hours before serving so the ingredients can marinate.

1 cup pimentos, chopped
1 6½-ounce jar marinated artichokes, chopped
¾ cup green olives, chopped
1 cup parsley, chopped
½ cup black Greek olives, pitted, chopped
½ pound Jarlsberg cheese, grated
½ cup capers

1. Mix all ingredients in food processor, except capers and cheese. Pulse to mix only until everything is chopped.
2. Stir in grated cheese and capers. Keep refrigerated.

Makes 4½ cups.

Do not let them sell you tamales made of goat meat.

Mint Oregano Pesto

Once you learn the basics of making pesto, the ideas for new combinations just keep coming - this one is great served with lamb.

1 cup fresh mint
1 cup fresh parsley
1 cup fresh oregano
5 garlic cloves
Peel of 1 lemon
½ cup olive oil
½ cup walnuts or pine nuts
1 teaspoon pepper
½ teaspoon salt

1. Measure all ingredients into food processor. Process until ingredients are thoroughly chopped.
2. Refrigerate or freeze.

Makes ¾ cup.

Sun-dried Tomato Pesto

I love to use Sun-dried tomatoes - and this is one of my favorite recipes to have on hand in my fridge. I like to mix it into butter for picnics - as a last minute topping for soups - toss it into hot pasta - pour over cream cheese for parties. Make some and let your creativity flow!

½ cup sun-dried tomatoes, softened in hot water, and drained
¾ cup walnuts, toasted
1 cup fresh basil
¾ cup olive oil
¾ cup Parmesan cheese, grated
6 garlic cloves
1 teaspoon pepper, freshly ground
Salt to taste

1. Measure all ingredients into food processor. Process until ingredients are thoroughly chopped. Taste for salt.
2. Refrigerate or freeze.

Makes 1½ cups.

Pesto Butter

I like to serve flavored butters next to a platter of sliced ham and turkey, and a basket of homemade bread. I mold mine into a heart shape and put a pretty flower and an herb sprig to dress it up for a party!

This is also a great idea for gift-giving. Pack pesto into a pretty jar, tie with a ribbon and then present it with a loaf of freshly baked bread!

1 pound butter
1½ tablespoons sun-dried tomatoes
½ cup Parmesan cheese, grated
¼ cup walnuts, toasted
½ cup fresh basil, chopped
¼ cup olive oil

1. Place butter in food processor. Process until smooth and creamy.
2. Add remaining ingredients and pulse just until mixed.
3. Mold into desired shape and chill.

Makes 2½ cups.

Lemon Olive Oil

We, in America, are beginning to catch on to a long standing custom of the Italians. More often than not, olive oil appears on the table in place of butter. We have found this recipe to be the perfect complement to our Tuscan bread.

Zest of 2 lemons
1 cup extra virgin olive oil
Rosé peppercorns (optional)

1. Peel zest from 2 lemons with potato peeler.
2. Crush with mortar and pestle until lemon zests are bruised. Add to olive oil.
3. Add peppercorns for color (optional).
4. Let set for 3 or 4 days before serving.

Makes 1 cup.

Jalapeño-Garlic Mayo

In our family, we can never have enough jalapeños or garlic! This mayo really dresses up a roasted chicken sandwich and it's fantastic on hamburgers!

4 garlic cloves
3 eggs
1 teaspoon salt
½ teaspoon pepper
1 tablespoon fresh lemon juice
2 tablespoons apple cider vinegar
2 tablespoons onion
2½ cups oil
2 tablespoons pickled jalapeños, sliced
3 tablespoons fresh cilantro

1. Combine all ingredients except oil, jalapeño slices, and cilantro in a food processor or blender. Process until finely chopped and well blended.
2. With machine running, slowly add oil, allowing the mayo to thicken as the oil is added.
3. Add jalapeño slices and cilantro and pulse 10 to 12 times so flakes of color will show.
4. Cover and refrigerate. It will keep up to five days.

Makes 3 cups.

Nadie sabe lo que contiene la olla,
nomás la cuchara que la menea.

Roasted Garlic Mayo with Sun-dried Tomatoes

Roasted Garlic (see Index) and sun-dried tomatoes add a unique flavor to this mayo - it's an exciting way to accent any sandwich!

1 green onion
3 tablespoons parsley
3 eggs
1 tablespoon Roasted Garlic (see Index)
2 tablespoons balsamic vinegar
2 teaspoons Dijon mustard
1 teaspoon salt
1 teaspoon pepper
2½ cups canola oil
2 tablespoons sun-dried tomatoes, minced

1. Combine all ingredients except oil and sun-dried tomatoes in a food processor or blender. Process until finely chopped and well blended.

2. With machine running, slowly add oil, allowing the mayo to thicken as the oil is added.

3. Stir in sun-dried tomatoes.

4. Cover and refrigerate. It will keep up to five days.

Makes 2¼ cups.

No one knows what is in the pot except the spoon that stirs the contents.

Curried Chutney Mayo

Delicious when used as a sandwich spread - especially with ham or smoked turkey - a slice of pineapple is a great addition!

2 whole eggs
1 egg yolk
1 teaspoon pepper
1 teaspoon salt
2 teaspoons curry powder
2 tablespoons vinegar
2 tablespoons lemon juice
2½ cups oil
2 to 3 tablespoons chutney

1. Combine all ingredients except oil and chutney in a food processor or blender. Process until well blended.
2. With machine running, slowly add oil, allowing mayo to thicken as oil is added.
3. Stir in chutney.
4. Cover and refrigerate. It will keep up to five days.

Makes 2½ cups.

Blender Hollandaise Sauce

Making hollandaise need never be a mystery to you again. Surprise someone you love on their special day with Eggs Benedict served in bed!

4 egg yolks
½ teaspoon salt
1 tablespoon lemon juice
Dash of Tabasco sauce
¼ pound butter, melted

1. Put the egg yolks, salt, lemon juice and Tabasco into blender jar. Cover and blend for about 30 seconds.
2. Continue blending and pour butter into jar in a steady stream until mixture is completely blended and thick.
3. Keep warm in bowl over hot water. Do not let the water boil.

Makes ¾ cup.

Horseradish Sauce

A great sauce to serve with slices of rare tenderloin or flank steak. Also, great spread on buttered bread slices for a roast beef sandwich. The ultimate addition would be arugula in place of lettuce!!

½ yellow onion, chopped
4 ounces horseradish
3 cups mayonnaise
1 teaspoon Worcestershire sauce

1. Place onion in food processor and pulse until onion is very finely minced and juicy. (This step gives a really good flavor to the sauce.)

2. Add other ingredients to onion and process until just combined and creamy.

Makes 3½ to 4 cups

Bechamel Sauce

I use this sauce to make the Seafood Lasagna (see Index). It's also just a nice basic recipe for cheese sauces, or creamed chicken, or seafood.

¼ cup butter
⅓ cup flour
¼ teaspoon salt
⅛ teaspoon nutmeg
¼ teaspoon white pepper
1¾ cups milk

1. Melt butter in saucepan. Add flour, salt, nutmeg and white pepper and cook, stirring over low medium heat for 2 to 3 minutes.

2. Add milk, and continue to cook, stirring constantly with whisk until sauce is thick and creamy, about 5 minutes.

Makes 2 cups.

Peach Tree Lemon Sauce

½ cup butter (not margarine)
4 eggs
2 cups sugar
½ cup plus 2 tablespoons fresh lemon juice, strained
1 tablespoon cornstarch
1 tablespoon lemon zest

1. Melt butter in non-aluminum saucepan on low heat.
2. Using a blender or food processor, blend eggs, sugar, lemon juice and cornstarch. Add to melted butter and cook on low heat, stirring constantly. Cook until mixture is thick and bubbly, about 8 minutes.
3. Remove from heat and add lemon zest. Serve warm or cold.

Makes about 2 cups. Keeps forever.

Crème Fraîche

I like to use Crème Fraîche on top of warm fruit cobblers or shortcakes. It is very smooth and creamy, and tastes a little bit lighter than sour cream. It's also very good when used to garnish soups and enchiladas!

2 cups whipping cream
4 tablespoons buttermilk

1. Pour cream into a glass container and stir in the buttermilk.
2. Cover the mixture and place in a draft-free area of your kitchen.
3. Do not disturb for 8 to 12 hours when mixture will be thick and the consistency of sour cream. Store in refrigerator.

Makes 2 cups.

Cookies

Lemon Thumbprint Cookies

I like to serve these on cookie platters for receptions - they are light and fresh tasting - pretty when garnished with violet blossoms or pink geranium leaves.

1 cup butter, melted
2 cups flour
¼ cup sugar
Pinch of salt
1 cup blanched almonds, chopped
2 teaspoons almond extract
1 cup Peach Tree Lemon Sauce (½ recipe) (see Index)

1. Preheat oven to 300 degrees.

2. In a bowl, mix all of the ingredients together until they are well-combined.

3. Roll the dough into teaspoon size balls and place on ungreased cookie sheet. Make thumbprints in the balls and bake for 30 minutes until light brown.

4. After the cookies have cooled, put some lemon sauce into the thumbprint.

Makes 3 dozen.

Lemon Amarettos

A moist lemon bar with a light almond flavor.

¾ cup butter, softened
¾ cup light brown sugar, packed
¼ cup white sugar
½ teaspoon almond extract
1 teaspoon amaretto
2 eggs
Zest and juice of 1 lemon
1¼ cups flour
½ teaspoon salt
½ cup sliced almonds, toasted
Powdered sugar

1. Preheat oven to 350 degrees.
2. In a mixing bowl, stir together the butter, sugars, almond extract, amaretto, eggs, lemon zest and juice until creamy.
3. Stir in flour, salt and almonds.
4. Pour the dough into a greased 8" x 8" baking pan. Bake for 20 to 30 minutes. After the bars are baked, sift a generous coating of powdered sugar on top. Let the bars cool before cutting.

Makes 16 bars.

Lemon Biscotti

Remember my good friends, Sally and Ottis Layne who I mention in the first cookbook as having a tradition of afternoon tea dates (Eccles Cake recipe) - well, they are still having their tea date, and the Biscotti is their latest favorite teatime treat. I find them to be great in the afternoon (anytime!) with cappuccino, too.

½ cup slivered almonds, toasted
½ cup butter
¾ cup sugar
2 eggs
2 tablespoons lemon juice
Zest of 1 lemon
1¾ cups flour
1½ teaspoons baking powder
¼ cup oats
¼ teaspoon salt

1. Place nuts in a shallow pan and bake in a preheated 325 degree oven until golden brown, about 8 to 10 minutes. Let cool.

2. In a mixing bowl cream butter and sugar until light and fluffy. Beat in eggs, lemon juice and zest. In a bowl combine flour, baking powder, oats and salt. Combine with creamed mixture, mixing until blended. Fold in almonds.

3. Divide dough in half. Place on greased and floured baking sheet and form into two logs about ½" thick, 1½" wide and 12" long, spacing them at least 2" apart. Bake in the middle of a preheated 325 degree oven for 25 minutes or until a light golden brown.

4. Transfer from the baking sheet to a rack and let cool 5 minutes. Place on a cutting board. With a serrated knife slice diagonally at a 45 degree angle about ½" thick. Lay the slices flat on the baking sheet and return to the oven for 10 minutes, turning them over once, to dry slightly. Let cool on a rack. Store in a tightly covered container.

Makes 3½ dozen.

Snickerdoodles

Everyone loves snickerdoodles - they revive our childhood memories!

1 cup butter, softened
2¼ cups sugar
2 eggs
¼ cup milk
1 teaspoon vanilla
3¾ cups flour
½ teaspoon baking soda
½ teaspoon cream of tartar
1 tablespoon cinnamon

1. Preheat oven to 375 degrees.

2. In mixing bowl, beat butter with 2 cups sugar until fluffy. Add eggs, milk and vanilla and beat thoroughly.

3. Add dry ingredients and mix until thoroughly combined.

4. Form the dough into tablespoon-size balls. Roll them in a mixture of cinnamon and ¼ cup sugar. Place cookies on ungreased cookie sheet.

5. Bake for 8 to 10 minutes or until they begin to look crinkly on top.

Makes 5 dozen.

Butterscotch Pecan Cookies

These cookies must be stirred by hand. The brown sugar and pecan combination makes this a delicious cookie!

1 cup butter, softened
2 cups brown sugar, packed
1 teaspoon vanilla
2 egg
3 cups flour
1 teaspoon salt
1 teaspoon baking powder
½ teaspoon baking soda
1½ cups pecans, coarsely chopped

1. Preheat oven to 350 degrees.
2. Beat the softened butter with the sugar and vanilla until creamy. Add the egg and mix well.
3. Combine the dry ingredients and mix into the dough. Stir in the pecans.
4. Drop by spoonful onto ungreased cookie sheets. Bake for 12 to 14 minutes. The cookies will be done when they are light brown.

Makes 4 dozen.

Note: Refrigerate the dough before baking to keep cookies from spreading.

Almond Heart Tea Cookies

A wonderful teatime cookie - very pretty and "not too sweet"!

3 egg yolks
⅔ cup sugar
½ teaspoon vanilla
½ teaspoon lemon extract
1¼ plus 1 cups almonds, very finely ground
¼ teaspoon baking powder

1. Preheat oven to 400 degrees.
2. Measure the first four ingredients into a bowl and beat well. Stir in 1¼ cups of the almonds and baking powder and mix thoroughly.
3. Spread the remaining cup of ground almonds on a counter top and knead them into the cookie dough. Wrap the dough in plastic and refrigerate for an hour or until it is cold.
4. Roll out the cookie dough on a counter top sprinkled with a little sugar, to about ¼" thickness. Use a small heart-shaped cookie cutter and bake on ungreased cookie sheet. They may be baked on a lightly greased cookie sheet for easier removal but they will spread more on a greased sheet.
5. Bake for about 8 minutes or until light brown.

Note: These cookies would also be wonderful with Powdered Sugar Glaze or Chocolate Glaze (see Index). You may need to cut the sugar in the recipe down to ½ cup if you use a powdered sugar glaze.

Makes 2½ dozen.

Good Ol' Fashioned Sugar Cookies

Lemonade is perfect with these in the summertime. We like to make a big batch of these because they're great cookies to have on hand and they freeze well.

1 cup butter, softened
1 cup canola oil
1 cup sugar
1 cup powdered sugar
2 eggs
1 teaspoon vanilla
4 cups flour
1 teaspoon cream of tartar
1 teaspoon baking soda
1 teaspoon salt

1. Preheat oven to 350 degrees.
2. Using a spoon, cream the butter with the oil and sugars. Add the eggs and vanilla and mix well by hand.
3. Stir in the dry ingredients. Cover the dough and chill until it is cold.
4. Roll into tablespoon size balls and place them on greased cookie sheets. Use the bottom of a glass to flatten the cookies. First, butter the bottom of the glass, dip it in sugar, then press the cookies.
5. Bake for 15 to 18 minutes until golden.

Makes about 8 dozen.

Pecan Shortbread Cookies

Equally good on picnics or at tea parties!

1¼ cups butter
1¼ cups brown sugar
2 teaspoons vanilla
2½ cups flour
1½ teaspoons salt
½ cup oats
⅓ cup pecans, chopped

1. Preheat oven to 325 degrees.
2. In a mixing bowl, cream butter and sugar. Add vanilla and blend thoroughly. Combine flour, salt and oats and gradually add to creamed mixture.
3. Stir in pecans and form into small balls using about 1 tablespoon batter each. Flatten ball with your hand and bake on ungreased cookie sheet for 15 to 20 minutes. Bake these in the middle of the oven.

Makes 3 dozen.

Fredericksburg Strudel Squares

I created these for a food class at the first Food and Wine Festival here in Fredericksburg. I wanted to feature the wonderful Peach Amaretto Pecan Preserves made by Fischer and Wieser of Fredericksburg. You can substitute a good quality of peach or apricot preserves if this is not available in your area.

2 10-ounce jars Peach Amaretto Pecan Preserves
2 cups pecans, chopped and roasted
1/2 pound filo pastry
1 cup butter, melted
12 ounces cream cheese, softened
1/4 cup peach syrup or honey
2 tablespoons Amaretto (or to taste)

1. Preheat oven to 375 degrees.

2. Combine preserves and pecans in a bowl and set aside. Brush a 9" x 13" glass baking dish with melted butter.

3. Place 10 filo leaves in the dish, brushing each of them with melted butter. Spread the cream cheese evenly over the 10 leaves. Spread ½ of the jam mixture over the cream cheese. Cover with 3 more leaves, each brushed with butter. Spread on the remaining jam mixture. Place the remaining leaves, each brushed with melted butter, on top.

4. Cut the strudel into squares or diamonds before baking. Bake 45 minutes, or until pastry is light brown. Remove from oven and allow to cool.

5. Brush top with a glaze of peach syrup or honey thinned with desired amount of Amaretto. Allow strudel squares to set for about 4 hours or overnight.

Makes 24.

Liebe macht blind.

Apricot Squares

The apricot preserves make these squares look like sparkling jewels on a cookie platter - and they are every bit as good as they appear!

1 cup butter
1 cup sugar
1 egg yolk
2 cups flour
¾ cup walnuts, chopped and toasted
1 18-ounce jar apricot jam or preserves

1. Preheat oven to 350 degrees.

2. In a large bowl cream together butter and sugar. Add egg yolk and mix well.

3. Stir in flour. Add nuts and blend well. Dough will be soft.

4. Divide dough in half. Spread half the dough evenly in a 9" x 13" baking dish. Cover with apricot jam.

5. Drop remaining dough by spoonfuls over jam, spreading carefully to the edges with a knife.

6. Bake for 40 to 45 minutes or until top is golden.

7. Remove from oven. Cool slightly, then cut into 1½" squares.

Makes 35.

Love is blind.

Aunt Mella's Italian Icebox Cookies

Tina discovered and rescued this recipe from my mother's old cookbook. Before she added the anise seed and pine nuts, they were just a nice basic cookie. Here you have the perfect finishing touch when serving Italian food. Also a delightful tea cookie!

½ cup butter, softened
⅔ cup sugar
½ teaspoon vanilla
1 egg
1⅓ cups flour
½ teaspoon baking powder
¼ teaspoon salt
¼ cup pine nuts
Anise seed

1. Preheat oven to 400 degrees.
2. In mixing bowl, cream butter, sugar and vanilla. Add egg.
3. Stir in flour, baking powder and salt. Stir well and add pine nuts. Form dough into roll - 1½" in diameter. Wrap dough in wax paper and refrigerate for 2 hours or overnight.
4. Slice dough into ½" thick cookies. Sprinkle with anise seed and bake for 8 to 10 minutes until lightly browned.

Makes 2 dozen.

El amór es ciego pero los vecinos no.

Bizcochos
Pedregon Wedding Cookies

Hector's aunt made these to serve at our wedding. It's the only recipe I own that uses pure lard - but the cookie is so delicious as it is, I wouldn't dream of changing it. I like to cut them into different sizes of star shapes - they make a delicious finish on a Mexican buffet.

3 cups sifted flour
1½ teaspoons baking powder
½ teaspoon salt
½ pound pure lard
1 cup sugar
1 teaspoon anise seeds
1 egg
2 tablespoons brandy
2 teaspoons cinnamon

1. Preheat oven to 350 degrees.
2. Sift flour with baking powder and salt.
3. Cream lard with ¾ cup sugar and anise seeds by hand or with electric mixer at medium speed. Beat egg until light and fluffy and add to the cream mixture.
4. Add flour mixture and brandy (use only enough brandy to form a stiff dough) and mix until well blended.
5. Knead dough lightly and pat or roll to ¼" or ½" thickness. Cut into fancy shapes. Generously sprinkle tops of cookies with a mixture of ¼ cup sugar and cinnamon.
6. Bake for 10 minutes or until very lightly browned.

Makes 3 to 4 dozen cookies, depending on the size.

Love is blind but not the neighbors.

Chocolate Crunch Cookies

Tina made up these cookies for her friend who loves soft chocolate chip cookies and Nestle Crunch Bars - the combination is perfect.

1½ cups soft butter, not melted
⅔ cup sugar
1 cup packed brown sugar
4 teaspoons vanilla
3 eggs
3 cups flour
1 teaspoon soda
1 teaspoon salt
1 cup chocolate chips
2 cups Nestle Crunch Bar, coarsely chopped (two 5-ounce giant bars)

1. Preheat oven to 350 degrees.

2. Cream the butter, sugars, vanilla and eggs. Add the flour, soda and salt. Stir in the chocolate chips and crunch bar.

3. Drop the dough by the spoonful onto ungreased cookie sheets. Bake for 12 to 14 minutes. The cookies will be done when they are light brown.

Makes 4 dozen cookies.

Collins Chocolate Cookies, Apricot Squares,
Collins Ranger Cookies, Super-Chocolicious Cookies,
Goat Cheese Pesto Tea Sandwiches and Lemonade

Mimi's Fudge

My mother's fudge recipe - very easy and it always works! For special occasions, cut with a small heart-shaped cutter!

3 cups semi-sweet chocolate chips
1 can sweetened condensed milk
Dash of salt
1 cup nuts
2 teaspoons vanilla

1. Melt together in microwave all ingredients except nuts and vanilla.

2. Stir in nuts and vanilla. Spread into 8" x 8" buttered pan.

3. Refrigerate about 2 hours until firm. Store at room temperature. Cut into desired shape.

Makes 16 squares.

Brownies for My Brother

These are the brownies that I baked for my "little" brother, Jeep, back home in Medina. He was the first choco-holic I'd ever known. He would hide cans of Nestle's Quick in his room for emergency snack attacks. Jeep loved these brownies and I made them every time I needed to make 'brownie' points with him!

1 cup butter
4 squares unsweetened baking chocolate
4 eggs
2 cups sugar
1 teaspoon vanilla
1 cup flour
¾ cup chocolate chips
¾ cup walnuts or pecans

1. Preheat oven to 350 degrees.

2. Melt the butter and chocolate together over low heat while stirring constantly. (Or melt them in a microwave, about 3 to 4 minutes on medium).

3. In a mixing bowl, beat the eggs until thick and lemon colored. Add sugar and vanilla and mix well.

4. Stir in the melted butter and chocolate to the mixture and beat again. Then mix in the flour. Stir in chocolate chips and walnuts or pecans.

5. Pour the butter into a greased 9" x 13" baking pan. Bake for 20 to 25 minutes, until a toothpick inserted in the center comes out clean. Be careful not to overbake so the brownies will be fudgy.

6. Get ready to receive your brownie points!

Makes 16.

The Peach Tree Chocolate Brownies

We use these for our Brownie Delight dessert in the Tea Room. We are including the recipe in this edition of the cookbook because it is a necessary ingredient for the White Chocolate Brownie Cheesecake and Kahlua Bars (see Index). For bridal brunches, we stencil a heart with powdered sugar on each individual brownie.

4 eggs
1½ cups sugar
2 teaspoons vanilla
1 cup melted butter or margarine
1½ cups Ghirardelli sweetened ground chocolate (no substitutes)
1½ cups flour
½ teaspoon baking powder
½ teaspoon salt
1 cup chopped walnuts or pecans

1. Using a spoon, combine eggs with sugar and vanilla. Add butter or margarine.

2. Mix ground chocolate with flour, baking powder, and salt. Stir into egg mixture. Add nuts.

3. Spread into a greased 9" x 13" pan, and bake in a preheated 350 degree oven for 30 to 35 minutes. Cool.

Makes 15 large or 60 small.

Chocolate-Peanut Butter Shortbread

The chocolate and peanut butter together make this a very rich bar cookie that's not too sweet - delicious to serve anytime.

Chocolate Shortbread:
    1 cup butter, softened
    ¾ cup sugar
    ⅓ cup unsweetened cocoa
    1 teaspoon vanilla
    2 cups flour

1. In a bowl, cream together the butter, sugar, cocoa and vanilla. Mix in the flour until smooth. Set aside.

Peanut Butter Layer:
    1 cup butter, softened
    ¼ cup crunchy peanut butter
    1 cup sugar
    1 egg yolk
    1 teaspoon vanilla
    1⅓ cups flour
    1 cup oats
    ½ cup salted, dry-roasted peanuts, chopped fine

1. Preheat oven to 300 degrees.

2. Cream the butter, peanut butter, and sugar together. Add the egg yolk and vanilla. Mix in the flour and oats.

3. Grease a 9" x 13" baking pan. Pat half of the Chocolate Shortbread into the pan. This will be a thin layer. Carefully put all of the Peanut Butter layer over the chocolate. Make the top layer with the rest of the Chocolate Shortbread. Spread it evenly over the peanut butter layer.

4. Sprinkle the peanuts over the shortbread and gently pat them into the shortbread.

5. Bake for about an hour. Check the shortbread after 45 minutes. The shortbread will be done when the sides look dry. Cut into squares while still hot. Let the shortbread cool before taking it out of the pan.

Makes 32 squares.

Super-Chocolicious Cookies

Tina tries to hide these special cookies in the freezer after she makes them. She and Helana like 'em so much they eat them straight from the freezer - yes, FROZEN!

¾ cup butter, softened
¾ cup sugar
¼ cup dark brown sugar, packed
½ cup light brown sugar, packed
2 ounces unsweetened baking chocolate, melted
2 teaspoons vanilla
1 egg
2 cups flour
1 teaspoon baking soda
1 teaspoon salt
½ cup pumpkin seeds, toasted lightly
½ cup pecans, coarsely chopped and toasted
1 cup semi-sweet chocolate chips

1. Preheat oven to 350 degrees.

2. Cream the butter with the sugars until light. Add the melted chocolate, vanilla and egg. Mix thoroughly.

3. Stir in the flour, baking soda, and salt. Then, add the pumpkin seeds, pecans, and chocolate chips.

4. Roll into tablespoon size balls and softly press down. Bake on ungreased cookie sheets for 10 to 14 minutes depending on how you like your cookies, soft or crispy.

Makes about 2½ dozen.

White Chocolate Almond Cookies

These dark moist chocolate cookies are filled with bits of white chocolate and almonds. Great served with coffee.

½ cup butter, soft
1 cup sugar
1 egg
½ teaspoon vanilla extract
½ teaspoon almond extract
⅓ cup unsweetened cocoa
1½ cups flour
½ teaspoon salt
½ teaspoon soda
1 teaspoon instant coffee
⅔ cup almonds, coarsely chopped and toasted
⅔ cup white chocolate chips
Powdered sugar

1. Preheat oven to 350 degrees.
2. Cream the butter with the sugar until light. Beat in egg, extracts, and the cocoa. Add the flour, salt, soda and coffee. Finally, mix in the almonds and chips.
3. Roll teaspoon-size dough in powdered sugar so that the dough has a thick layer of sugar. Place the cookies on ungreased cookie sheet and bake for 15 to 20 minutes.

Makes about 2 dozen.

Wie die Alten sungen so zwitschern die Jungen.

Miss Maribeth's Cookies

Our son, Carlos, brought this recipe home from school - his teacher used to serve them to her class. Every now and then, he reminds Tina to make them for him - they're still his favorite!

1 cup butter, softened
1 cup sugar
1 cup brown sugar
1 teaspoon vanilla
2 eggs
3 cups flour
1 teaspoon salt
1 teaspoon baking soda
2 cups chocolate chips

1. Preheat oven to 325 degrees.
2. In a mixing bowl, cream the soft butter, sugars and vanilla with a spoon. Beat in the eggs. Combine the flour, salt and baking soda and mix well. Mix in the chocolate chips.
3. Roll the dough into tablespoon-size balls and flatten with the palm of your hand.
4. Bake on an ungreased cookie sheet for 8 to 10 minutes.

Makes 3 dozen.

As the old ones sing— so whistle the younger ones.

Collins Ranger Cookies

Tina found this recipe tucked away in an old Collins family cookbook - it's a really good "light" cookie.

1 cup oats, finely ground*
1 cup butter, softened
⅔ cup white sugar
⅔ cup brown sugar, packed
1 teaspoon vanilla
2 eggs
2 cups flour
1 teaspoon baking soda
½ teaspoon baking powder
½ teaspoon salt
1 cup rolled oats
2 cups rice crispies cereal
1 cup coconut, flaked
1 cup raisins
1 cup pecans, chopped and toasted

1. Preheat oven to 350 degrees.
2. Beat the butter with the sugars and vanilla until light. Add the eggs and mix well.
3. Measure the rest of the ingredients into the bowl except for the raisins and the pecans and mix well. Then add the raisins and pecans.
4. Form the cookie dough into balls and bake on ungreased cookie sheets for 10 to 12 minutes.

Makes 4 dozen.

*Note: In a food processor or blender, process oats briefly, and set aside.

Whole Wheat Chocolate Chip Cookies

Tina is really into exercising and nutrition and was trying to come up with a "healthy" chocolate chip cookie - by using whole wheat flour. I'm not sure how "healthy" it is - but it sure is good!

½ cup butter, softened
½ cup canola oil
½ cup white sugar
½ cup brown sugar
2 teaspoon vanilla
2 eggs
2 cups whole wheat flour
½ cup white flour
1 teaspoon soda
1 teaspoon salt
1 cup walnuts, chopped and toasted
1 cup chocolate chips

Tip: There is a big difference in these cookies if mixed by hand. Using a mixer dries them out too much.

1. Preheat oven to 350 degrees.
2. Beat the butter and oil with the sugars. Add the vanilla and eggs and beat well.
3. Stir in the dry ingredients, then the walnuts and chocolate chips.
4. Drop by the spoonful onto ungreased cookie sheets. Bake for 10 to 12 minutes. The cookies will be done when they are light brown.

Makes 3 dozen.

Note: Try using raisins instead of chocolate chips for another good cookie.

Collins Chocolate Cookies

One of Tina's outstanding chocolate creations - put some in your freezer for later - before they disappear!

1 cup butter, softened
1 cup sugar
1 cup brown sugar, packed
4 teaspoons vanilla
2 eggs
1 cup unsweetened cocoa
1 teaspoon cinnamon
3 cups flour
1 teaspoon baking soda
1 teaspoon salt
4 tablespoons brewed coffee
1 cup chocolate chips
1 cup Hershey candy bar, chopped
1½ cups walnuts, chopped and toasted

1. Preheat oven to 350 degrees.
2. Cream the butter with the sugars until mixed well. Add the vanilla and eggs until light and fluffy.
3. Stir in the cocoa and cinnamon.
4. Mix the flour with the soda and salt and add to the batter. Mix in the coffee with the flour.
5. Stir in the chocolate chips, candy and nuts.
6. Roll into tablespoon-size balls and place onto ungreased cookie sheets.
7. Bake for 8 to 10 minutes. Watch carefully since these burn easily.

Makes 4 dozen.

Oatmeal Raisin Chews

So easy to make and taste tempting, too!

1½ cups raisins
3 tablespoons brandy
1 cup butter, soft, but not melted
¾ cup sugar
¾ cup brown sugar
1 teaspoon vanilla
1 egg
1½ cups flour
1 cup oats, finely ground*
1 cup old-fashioned whole oats
1 teaspoon baking soda
1 teaspoon salt

1. Soak the raisins in the brandy, which has been heated. Cover with plastic wrap to allow the raisins to plump. Set aside.

2. In a large bowl, mix the butter with the sugars until the dough is light. Add the vanilla and egg and mix well.

3. Combine the flour, oats, baking soda, and salt. Stir into the dough. Add the raisins.

4. Refrigerate the dough for an hour. Preheat the oven to 350 degrees. Measure the dough into tablespoon-size balls and flatten slightly. Bake the cookies on greased cookie sheets for 8 to 12 minutes.

Makes 3 dozen.

Peach Chew Variation:
Substitute 1½ cups (8 ounces) chopped dried peaches for raisins and soak in brandy as above.

1½ cups pecans, chopped (optional)

*Note: In a food processor or blender, process oats briefly, and set aside.

Chewy Granola Bars

The sweetness of the granola in these bars will change the taste. If using a sweet granola, you may cut the sugar down to 1¼ cups.

½ cup soft butter
1¾ cups brown sugar, packed
2 eggs
1 teaspoon vanilla
¾ cup white flour
¾ cup whole wheat flour
2 teaspoons baking powder
1 teaspoon salt
1½ cups granola
½ cup nuts, coarsely chopped

1. Preheat oven to 350 degrees.
2. In a mixing bowl, combine the butter, brown sugar, eggs and vanilla. Beat with a spoon or whisk until light. Stir in the flours, baking powder and salt. Add the granola and nuts last.
3. Pour the batter into a greased 9" x 13" baking pan. Bake for about 25 minutes or until a toothpick comes out clean.

Makes 32.

Kahlua Bars
(A Triple-Decker Dessert)

We began with Peach Tree Brownies and added a layer of Kahlua icing and a thin fudgy topping - I think it's called gilding the brownie!! But, go for it...you only live once!

First Layer:
    1 recipe Peach Tree Brownies (see Index)

Second Layer:
    ½ cup butter, softened
    3 tablespoons Kahlua
    2 cups confectioner's sugar

Third Layer:
    6 ounces semi-sweet chocolate bits
    2 tablespoons butter

First Layer: Make brownies as directed. Cool and remove from pan in 1 piece onto tray.

Second Layer: Cream together all ingredients and spread evenly over the first layer. Cool until set.

Third Layer: Melt semi-sweet chocolate bits with butter over hot, **NOT BOILING**, water in a double boiler. Spread on top of the second layer. Cool until set. Cut into small-size squares. Freeze. Defrost and serve cool. Store in refrigerator.

Makes 16 to 24 bars.

Chris' Congo Bars

My cousin Chris, from Michigan, gave me this recipe when we were little girls. It has been in the Collins family a very long time.

1 cup melted butter
2½ cups brown sugar, packed
2½ cups flour
2½ teaspoons baking powder
½ teaspoons salt
3 eggs
1 cup pecans, chopped and toasted
1 cup chocolate chips
1 teaspoon vanilla

1. Preheat oven to 350 degrees.

2. Melt the butter and pour over the brown sugar. Let this set while you measure the flour, baking powder and salt into a bowl.

3. Add the eggs gradually to the butter mixture and beat well. Mix in the dry ingredients. Stir in the pecans, chocolate chips and vanilla.

4. Pour into a greased 9" x 13" baking pan. Bake for 30 to 40 minutes. When a toothpick comes out clean, the bars will be done. Let them cool before cutting.

Makes about 32 bars.

Orange-Pecan Chocolate Bars

The oranges and pecans make these a moist cookie. You should probable double this recipe so they'll last longer because they are so good!

½ cup butter, softened
1 cup light brown sugar, packed
2 teaspoons Grand Marnier
Zest from ½ orange
2 eggs
1 cup flour
¼ teaspoon salt
⅓ cup pecans, chopped and toasted
1 Hershey's Milk Chocolate Bar (1.55 ounces), chopped

1. Preheat oven to 350 degrees.

2. In an electric mixer, cream the butter and sugar until light and fluffy. This step is important for the bars to be light.

3. Add the Grand Marnier, zest and eggs. Again beat the mixture well.

4. Fold in the flour and salt. Add the pecans and Hershey Bar.

5. Pour the mixture into an 8" x 8" baking pan.

6. Bake for 25 to 35 minutes. The bars will be done when they are light brown on top or when a toothpick comes out clean. Cool before cutting.

Makes 16 bars.

Orange Glaze (optional):
    1 cup powdered sugar
    4 tablespoons frozen orange juice concentrate
    Enough milk to make a thick glaze.

When the bars have cooled for 10 minutes, the glaze can be spread on top.

Notes

_____

_____

_____

_____

_____

_____

_____

_____

_____

_____

_____

_____

_____

_____

Index